Executive Greed

Removing the Excessive Compensation Stigma

JOSEPH L. BOUNDS

DEDICATION

I give many thanks to God for providing unique insight into this book's research, its writing, and inspiration for achieving these results. Greatly appreciated are these gifts.

My wife Lynn stayed the course with her understanding and love while providing a sounding board and proofreading. I love you very much.

CONTENTS

1 PREFACE

This book builds upon the author's previous research of establishing a quantifiable metric for excessive compensation of executives and managers in publicly traded corporations. The heart of this text uses easy to understand language and examples to provide analysis of wage structures within 30 industries resulting in a large amount of evidence supporting this metric's definition. Additionally, there is evidence and data defining a metric for limiting management and executive bonuses. Together these form the basis for a new management compensation theory for developing limitations to remove the stigma of excessive executive compensation. There are many figures throughout this book illustrating the results of data analysis with these industries. These figures represent the data covering almost 42 million people within the United States' workforce. This book also establishes links to national level research on wage distributions in other counties thereby creating routes for national and international applications.

There are several reasons for writing this book. First, this provides an opportunity to expand research into quantitative methods applicable to defining excessive executive compensation. Second, this analysis broadens the original research to 30 industries and demonstrates wide applicability of these methods. Third, reducing excessive compensation can provide a huge, positive economic impact on corporate performance in nations around the world. Fourth, historically no quantifiable means existed to define excessive executive compensation based on quantitative income data, but previous research overcame this obstacle and this book provides additional reinforcement.

The economic impact of acting on this data has a huge potential for changing how companies assign compensation to executives and managers with resulting economic savings in many millions of dollars. Shareholders and other stakeholders of companies choosing to act on this information should find their assets in a better position to compete, domestically and internationally. These stakeholders will also be able to remove the negative stigma associated with media reporting of compensation amounts paid to executives in the form of annual salaries and bonuses by having a validated means to justify these amounts. The total effects of increased economic benefits through reducing the huge amount of overhead associated with senior executives and managers are difficult to evaluate because they reach into areas of social responsibility, ethical conduct, and among others, into domestic and international economic competitiveness. This book should create interesting discussion, thought, and evaluation when considering what your personal investments are paying for and what your money is actually doing. In this author's opinion, it should not finance the extravagant lifestyle of executives, but return better consumer products and improved shareholder dividends through stronger economic competition.

2 HISTORY AND MYTHS

A Brief History of the Corporation

The history of governing bodies incorporating organizations has roots extending back many centuries to the ancient Roman Republic. At this time, most people thought the world was flat and high tech was a horse drawn wagon. Moving ahead to the 14th and 15th centuries and beyond, monarchs in the European nations had learned the world was not flat, sought riches in newly discovered lands, and sometimes bestowed incorporation rights upon early universities, towns, and ecclesiastical groups setting out into this new frontier. The idea behind the corporate charter concept is to grant some rights of self-determination which entitle these groups to legal abilities beyond those of an average citizen. Along with this went the property of creating an element of immortality because incorporated organizations may exist long after individuals in the body granting incorporation as well as the original incorporated group have passed on.[1]

In 1776, the year of independence in the United States, Adam Smith described how a market economy functions in his book *The Wealth of Nations*. This volume possesses remarkable insight considering the technology of this time and there existing little technology to perform analysis on global economic conditions. Among many observations, he did see a problem with executives having unbridled access to corporate resources in bettering their own position.

The directors of such companies, however, being the managers rather of other people's money than of their own, it cannot well be expected, that they should watch over it with the same anxious vigilance with which the partners in a private copartnery frequently watch over their own, p. 941.[2]

State legislatures as early as the late eighteenth century established the beginning process of enacting laws to govern incorporation and enable the public in general to incorporate various groups. An appealing element to corporate investors was partial protection of their assets that, if the investment succeeded, would preserve them in perpetuity. Initially, one of the problems was that many people believed as Adam Smith and were fearful that executives running these organizations could be wasteful with their investments without obtaining anything in return.[3] Recent research by various individuals have reaffirmed the early fears experience by investors, so much so that it is noted that early legal mandates ruled the actions of self-serving corporate officers as invalid.[4]

Fiduciary duty is a legal concept that places trust with an individual as part of their employment and prevents self-serving employees from taking advantage of one's position and acting in self-interest to improve personal standing at the expense of their employer. In this concept, the employer is the *principle* and the employee acts as an *agent* on behalf of their employer.[5] One example of a breach of fiduciary responsibility would be contracting with a neighbor to do your yard maintenance. You provide equipment, fuel, and money in a petty cash box for expenses such as replacing gasoline and maintenance (assets). Fifty dollars per week is the agreed compensation. The neighbor thinks he can increase his income by using these assets to maintain several other neighborhood properties for additional pay. Thus, the neighbor takes advantage at the employer's expense, to further his own income, thus violating fiduciary responsibility and wasting the resources for personal gain.

Managers and corporate executives are agents and as such owe undivided loyalty to their employers, namely the owners or stockholders. Managers and executives are required in this context to limit their self-interests in a way that would not place themselves in a better position or take advantage of their employers. Existing laws require informing his or her employers when problems may act on this relationship and touch on fiduciary responsibilities. Another aspect of this relationship is that of compensating an agent for his or her actions when meeting the terms of employment.[6] Agents, as employees of companies, are compensated for their services.

Fiduciary responsibilities exist between managers and there are many executive titles, with the chief executive officer (CEO) being the highest position. Corporate bylaws may define the compensation level that a member of the board of directors receives as well as number of positions constituting a board. Another possible source for defining the elements of a corporate board's compensation is in results of shareholder meetings. Fiduciary requirements are also supposed to prohibit a board or other executives from acting in self-interest.[7] An interesting deviation from the principle of fiduciary responsibility was a move of the state legislature of Delaware, which has the most liberal corporation laws in the country, in adding Section 102(b)(7) to the state's General Incorporation Law. This legislation permits corporations chartered under Delaware's laws to change their charter of incorporation to permit waiving personal liability of directors in execution of fiduciary duties. In effect, this appears to remove accountability of a board of directors to investors and shareholders.[8]

The origin of boards of directors is in the need for a broader perspective constituting multiple backgrounds and experiences to improve oversight. Collective oversight based on a group's input many times can avoid the biases and limited experience that may originate from just one or two individuals. Within the responsibilities of a board is a fiduciary duty to monitor management on behalf of shareholders, provide counsel to management when formulating corporate strategies, and provide strategic corporate input as management addresses routine administrative requirements. Boards are not constantly in session, but meet only a few times during a year such as quarterly or semiannually to provide their cognitive output. Board personnel require social-psychological interactions for making critical decisions and maintaining effective communication. Maintaining an effective information exchange is crucial when deciding to approve or reject management initiatives, alter compensation levels, and renovate senior management membership. However, the cyclic nature of short-term board meetings followed by larger time gaps many times contributes to members failing to invest the required time to develop a deep, root cause understanding of a corporation's problems.[9]

The number of CEO's that are chairpersons of corporate boards fluctuates from time to time, but noted at one time to be as high as 74%. Chairing the board provides additional power and control over its actions and can result in entrenching a CEO to the point that a board's actions are limited and allow a pernicious methodology for remuneration.[10] This additional influence with a CEO in this position can also contribute to a biased viewpoint that slants observations toward those of his or her social grouping, refocuses consideration away from being a corporate employee, and adds to devaluing consumers or owners. Groupthink can develop within such a group and contribute to CEOs believing exorbitant compensation levels are a birthright.[11] These actions many times translate to create weak corporate governance and increase the agency problem between principles and agents to serve diverse interests other than those aligned with a principle's intent.

Investigation into corporate governance and CEO compensation levels with senior executive involvement reveals companies experiencing weak governance typically demonstrate higher CEO remuneration, and therefore higher overhead costs, than corporations with stronger and more independent boards.[12] There were many corporate scandals shortly after the turn of the millennium and research disclosed continued and widespread involvement of executives in earnings manipulation. This points to failure in the effective workings of corporate governance, absence of personal accountability in senior management, and executive's abuse of power to bring corporate boards to heel so they become unwilling to question senior management's initiatives.[13] These situations highlights greed at the senior executive levels even when executives within the United States are receiving higher levels of compensation than those in other countries where there are higher costs of living. This condition also feeds a lust for power as compensation amounts correlate with executive power over a corporate board.[14]

As a subset of a company's board of directors, compensation committees many times are comprised of executives that are internal and external to the organization. This relationship works to instill a bias toward self-interests resulting in supporting one another with a side effect of allocating personal benefits, strengthening power positions within established hierarchies, and resisting proposed changes that are contrary to what they believe. The reality is that boards cannot correct their governance problems as they have a root cause in systemic issues resulting from improper executive control over information and manipulation of board membership. The social and psychological forces that act in requiring a board to work together also work against basic system reforms in determining executive compensation.[15]

A key problem faced by all players in defining excessive compensation is how to define "excessive" in a meaningful way that subjugates compensation to a method of quantitative measurement. By many observations, the annual public outrage experienced with media announcements of multi-million dollar bonuses to corporate executives originates in wage compensation disparity between a majority of company or industry employees and the executives who are company employees. If a company compensates a worker with an industry average annual salary of $50,000, there is something fundamentally wrong with another employee receiving a salary in the millions and a bonus that is a multiple of this base salary. To put it in better perspective, an income of $1,000,000 after taxes would pay this individual $50,000 a year for 20 years or approximately half of a working career – a huge disparity for individuals making $50,000 or less. Except for two industries presented in this book whose average salaries were more than $50,000 and less than $54,000, the majority of workers from the remaining 28 industries falls far short of this $50,000 mark and indicates a disparity in compensation that is much greater.

This book presents an argument based on a quantitative data analysis of 30 industries and thousands of data points that illustrate some executive compensations are excessive. Repercussions of this analysis also reach into the international arena of wage compensation and therefore affect the economic achievement of corporations on a global scale. There is an additional need of comparative evaluation of current compensation practices against modern definitions of social responsibility and ethical corporate behavior. Two industries described later in this book provide statistical correlation to the lognormal statistical distribution which a number of researchers have linked to multiple countries. The significance of this link is that this analysis has an international impact on executive compensation and corporate economic performance.

Why should anyone care?

Public outcry always brings with it the attention of the Congress of the United States and other levels of elected officials who have responsibility to establish laws. The topic of excessive executive compensation falls into this arena by addressing public outcry at compensation that is wasteful when many companies have reduced their workforce personnel in record numbers to stay in business. Even in good times, it is wasteful and irresponsible to have more overhead costs than necessary.

Public and shareholder outrage has reached new heights when announcing multimillion-dollar bonuses for executives. In attempting to describe the magnitude of executive compensation levels, current levels of executive compensation can also be termed as gluttony. Senator (now President) Barack Obama once criticized executives and their uncontrolled helping of themselves to the corporate monetary cookie jar because they receive more in a day than the average worker is able to earn in a year.[16]

One of the difficult problems faced by the court system in the past is determining how to define what constitutes reasonable compensation and where does excessive compensation begin? This is no longer the case as research has defined a quantitative, data driven metric for defining excessive compensation and this book offers additional refinement on the subject. [17]

Because there are multiple district courts in the United States, each within its judicial authority has tackled the problem of defining excessive executive compensation with the result of creating multiple tests for defining reasonable compensation. An obvious problem with this methodology is multiple tests create multiple standards that complicate application with any reasonable level of effectiveness. [18] This multiple standard approach also creates complexity when trying to establish a universal standard that quantitatively defines a limit on reasonable compensation and therefore a threshold for where excessive executive compensation begins. Additional complications come about when realizing that the U.S. Treasury and tax code is missing a quantitative definition of what is reasonable and what is excessive when it comes to executive compensation levels. The use of a working, mathematical definition based on industry data establishes a quantitative boundary while creating an environment where enforcement would become possible.

The Myths

A long list of theories exits to define the observed

characteristics of establishing executive compensation levels and after review, there is a sense it is as though a group of people are observing some event from different locations and angles. Each individual has a different locational perspective than his or her counterparts and each expresses a different observation based on mental orientation and observation. Overall, these theories are missing the quantitative measure necessary to establish and derive a meaningful standard compensation level and fall far short of a metric defining excessive compensation. Even modern theories relating to atomic energy present equations to gauge how they function and define expected results. In a few cases when a compensation method is stated, the association is to a large value on the corporate balance sheets so that even if the reward is a small percentage, the outcome is great and not tied to how a majority of corporate or industry personnel receive compensation. The following are some of the more common theories, in brief, that describe executive compensation and I term these "the myths" because they offer no method of quantitative decision-making.

Agency Theory

A search of the literature on compensation theories shows the most prominent and generally accepted myth of how corporate boards and executives should interact with one another in setting compensation is Agency Theory. Financial economists and many others favor the concept of agency theory and the idea of arm's length contracting that goes along with it. This theory works on the assumption that shareholders provide guidance and input to a board of directors who use this information to bargain at arm's length with executives for services. Many people in the world of corporate boards, senior executives, and managers approve of this theory because of the justification provided them in their decisions when addressing compensation decisions to corporate shareholders, policy makers, and when challenged in courts. Superficially, this myth appears adequate, but on closer examination, many pitfalls become apparent. Managers, having their own self-serving interests at heart, would not normally be motivated to focus on increasing shareholder value. Likewise, it is naive to think corporate boards would also function this way. The challenge of aligning the interests of principle (corporate board) and agent (executive) is problematic and creates the *agency problem*. Lavishing benefits exceeding those specified in contracts on departing CEOs provides credible sources of evidence that there is a failure in arm's length contracting and agency theory in both theory and practice.[19]

Agency theory addresses the concept of one person contracting with another to perform some function or task and in doing so, the agent acts in the principle's primary interest. Because the agent has one set of objectives and incentives that motivate him or her and the principle possesses a differing set of objectives and incentives, agency theory indicates alignment of these elements is possible through altering compensation methods to bring both parties into agreement. Negotiation of these differences, in theory, creates an alignment of the agent's behavior with that of the principle to result in maximizing shareholder wealth.[20]

Agency theory originated in the early twentieth century and came about when owners shifted control of corporations to managers due to issuing public stock offerings to achieve growth that expanded companies into both multiple and diverse locations. As stated earlier, there are several problems with this arrangement, another of which is having a higher diversified group of shareholders that as a group possess multiple interests, all expecting management to disburse corporate profits. Management on the other hand is reluctant to distribute monetary resources because a reduction in any resource, especially money, creates a constraint on management's capacity to meet corporate growth and expansion goals. Management will strive to achieve growth in some form because, from an historical point of view, growth is a common metric to provide recognition for increased compensation, promotions, and power.[21]

Agency theory seeks to overcome the morally tempting situation of providing managers access to large corporate resources while having little ownership in the company they serve, in short, they have access to a piggy bank that is not theirs. This is the moral hazard problem and where extravagant opportunism could result. Executives and managers sometimes choose to exploit the principle-agent relationship by refusing to accept the risk associated with various employment situations in an attempt to increase compensation incentives.[22] Some researchers take the point of view that executive and CEO compensation appears to fall into the realm of irrational decision-making that puts executives in a position to extract wealth from a company without maximizing shareholder value.[23] Evaluating what this theory implies, it sounds very much like the executive is expected to behave in a dishonest, illegal way and somehow increasing the individual's pay makes him or her honest.

Current agency theory definitions do not allow an adequate methodology for establishing compensation thresholds. There exists a need for board members to evaluate reality and ask what the contribution / remuneration worth of an individual is within a public corporation. Rare are the actual observations of an executive who is the superb motivator, galactic corporate leader, walks on water without getting his or her feet wet, or superstar of management skill.[24] As the impact of the financial crisis deepened and Wall Street firms received massive government bailouts, the bonuses received by employees provoked widespread public outrage. Merril Lynch and American International Group ("AIG") were perceived as especially controversial. In 2009 Merril Lynch allocated $3.6 billion in bonuses to its employees and AIG paid $218 million in bonuses. President Barack Obama described Wall Street bonuses as "shameful."[25]

Managerial Power Theory

Managerial power theory is another myth on how executive compensation works and like a phoenix, tries to arise out of the ashes of agency theory to achieve an explanation. This myth does explain in some detail how power influences the increases in executive pay, but falls short in defining reasonable or excessive compensation for executives and senior managers.

Interrelationships between executives and board members constrain the principles of arm's length bargaining when it becomes apparent that hiring a CEO effectively puts this person in a position to fire the board members that do the hiring. Professionally and financially, the situation can become one where it is better to cooperate with a CEO's wishes than to oppose them. Managerial power theory does offer a logical explanation of wielding power to limit information access to board members, and strong-arm tactics in the award of extravagant compensation, bonus, and separation packages.[26]

Salary and Skill Relationships

Moving from the area of compensation theories and myths takes us into the area of arguments for compensation based on salary and skills. Research indicates the levels of optimism when selecting a new CEO has basis in a belief system where a new executive's success and skills will successfully transfer to their new position with an end result of increasing stock dividends. This belief is partially true and partially myth. The skills needed to invoke a vision, create motivation, and maintain budgetary oversight usually transfer well between organizations, but skill sets idiosyncratic to processes and management systems can be like trying to swap a professional football player with a star competitive swimmer and can create a difficult transitional fit for an organization. It is important to see beyond pedigree for senior managers that graduate from esteemed management schools when hoping to score a super star CEO or other senior manager. Organizational compatibility combined with portable skills are key factors contributing to success within an organization.[27]

Increased company profitability cannot be a means to justify executive compensation and bonuses. Contrary to corporate profit increases, the income of CEOs grew 9.5% in 2002, 15% in 2003, 30% in 2004, and 130% from 2005 to 2006. The year 2006 saw an average CEO pay increase for the top 250 U.S. companies at 38% over 2005 and the market profitability for these companies did not remotely reach these results. Few Americans outside those executives receiving this type of preferential treatment experienced this type of pay increases. The economy did not grow 30% in 2004 and definitely did not grow 130% between 2005 and 2006. With these facts in mind, there appears little ground in justifying and defending huge salaries and bonuses paid to executives. If one were to compare these rates with the President of the United States, an average CEO becomes 62 times more productive and valuable because their compensation is 62 times greater.[28]

Another misleading argument executives like to utilize is pointing out how much organizational wealth they create. A reality check shows executives have little influence on which direction the organization ends up traveling. This is readily apparent with an examination of the stock market bubble late in the 20th century. Achievements of an organization require the concerted efforts of many people in many occupations. Therefore, it is not reasonable to credit wealth creation to one individual and many times not to a small group due to a limited span of control. Those in charge and agreeing with this false premise fail to notice the reverse situation when conditions go negative, there are losses on a balance sheet, and an executive is not screaming from the rooftops for a reduction in compensation.[29]

Prior research into compensation levels indicates there are important factors involved that include the industry where executives and managers are operating, the company itself as some are more in leader or dominating roles, and size of the corporation. However, when looking at a broader, international perspective, Japanese and British firms reward their executives and managers at a lower rate than observed in the United States. When taking this larger point of view, the revealing element is that there are lesser contributions directly related to a CEO's performance within a corporation and true outcomes more result from the overall contributions and dedication of employees.[30]

One of the arguments posed in the justification of senior manager and executive compensation is that of ability versus power. Executives like to claim they possess quantum leaps in ability over those below them in the corporate rank and file, but investigative research does not prove this out. As pointed out in the following quote, there is a slight increase in ability, but the levels of compensation received correlate to a much higher degree when compared to positional title. There is no justification of the vast sums senior managers and executives receive based on differences in ability when compared to the corporate workforce. These figures attribute a substantial part of the inequality of earnings to power differences. The most powerful jobs in the economy (the top one in a million) have power about 200 times the median level, and earnings about 100 times the median level, but are held by people with ability only 3-1/2 times the median level. The high earnings reflect the individual's ordinal position – the fact that he is at the top of the ability distribution – much more than the level of his ability, yet earnings do not reflect the economic value of ability.[31]

One of my interesting observations is that as an individual progresses up the corporate chain of command, the great increases in salary occur just by changing titles. The rise up the corporate ladder also reduces the direct interaction an individual has with those in the organization that are below him or her who are directly responsible for achieving goals against performance metrics. Individuals with direct reports who are directly responsible for outcomes may be several layers below. Simply put, individuals higher up on the organizational chart become more responsible for administration requirements, but there is no radical change in skills, education, or ability justifying the large percentages of pay received.

3 LET'S GET DICEY

Dice

     Dice are a great tool for review of how normal number distributions function. The following is a simple, short tutorial on some general statistics for those who have little background in how these numbers work, what they represent, and for individuals that may need to rub a little rust off these tools due to limited usage. This is not complicated and dice as a teaching tool provides familiarity because many people know these from many different types of games.

     Most people are familiar with dice and they come in many sizes and colors and may have pointed corners or more rounded ones to aid in easier rolling. One thing all dice have in common when used in this fashion is the number of spots on each of six sides range from one spot representing the number one to six spots for the number six. There are no blank sides so regardless of which side faces up, there is always a number represented. When rolling as a single or in a pair, there are specific possibilities to come up with a given number.

     Take two dice and label one die 1 as and the other as 2. When looking at possible combinations we can start with die 1. Because there are no blank sides, when rolling two dice the lowest possible number is 2. Die one must come up a 1 and die two must also come up with a 1 (1, 1), a double. No other combination is possible.

     When rolling to obtain a 3, die one can be a 1 and die two

must be a 2 (1, 2), changing die one to a 2 requires die two to become a 1 (2, 1), or two possibilities of obtaining a 3.

When going for a 4, die one may be a 1 in which case die two must be a 3 (1, 3). Changing die one to a 2 requires die two to become a 2 (2, 2), a double. Die one becoming a three requires die two to become 1 (3, 1). Thus, there are three possibilities for getting the number 4. Continuing this methodology out for all possible numbers results in the following combinations:

> 5: (1, 4), (2, 3), (3, 2), 4, 1)
> 6: (1, 5), (2, 4), (3, 3), (4, 2), (5, 1)
> 7: (1, 6), (2, 5), (3, 4), (4, 3), (5, 2), (6, 1)
> 8: (2, 6), (3, 5), (4, 4), (5, 3), (6, 2)
> 9: (3, 6), (4, 5), (5, 4), (6, 3)
> 10: (4, 6), (5, 5), (6, 4)
> 11: (5, 6), (6, 5)
> 12: (6, 6)

So why do we care about the possibilities of getting a particular number with dice when we are concerned with wage earnings within various industries? The answer is that the principles that we are interested in addressing for executive compensation are the same and just as easy to understand. To understand the average of a number set, ignore the above dice example for a moment and consider the following numbers and their total:

$$1+2+3+4+5+6+7+8+9+10+11+12 = 78.$$

There are 12 possible numbers so divide 78 by 12 and the answer is 6.5, which is the average or sometimes called the mean. If we were to add another large number, say 100, the total would become 178 and the average shifts to approximately 13.7. This demonstrates that large numbers and the resulting shifts do not represent the majority of data within an information set.

If we add up all the individual combinations for numbers on our dice, we get 36. Thus, we get one chance in 36, or 1/36 of obtaining a 2 (1, 1) or 0.0277778 = 2.78%, the same for a 12 (6, 6), and so on with the highest possibility, six combinations with a 7 or 6/36 = 0.1666667 or 16.67%.

We are not going to concern ourselves with the mechanics and mathematics of calculating a standard deviation as this is beyond the interest of this book, most of its readers, and is usually only of interest in statistics classes or process analysis. Important is the understanding that a standard deviation is a calculated value and many calculators and computer programs can generate this number. The standard deviation is just a number that indicates how much the data varies, nothing to get worried about here.

If we enter all the numbers by the frequency they occur for our dice into a calculator or computer program, a single 2, two 3s, three 4s and so on, it will tell us that the mean or average is 7 and the standard deviation (our calculated value) is 2.449.

If we enter all possible values on blocks, similar to children's alphabetical blocks, and stack them in order according to the number they represent, we obtain a result similar to Figure 1.

There are two basic types of statistical distributions providing a "bell curve." One is the lognormal distribution and the other is the

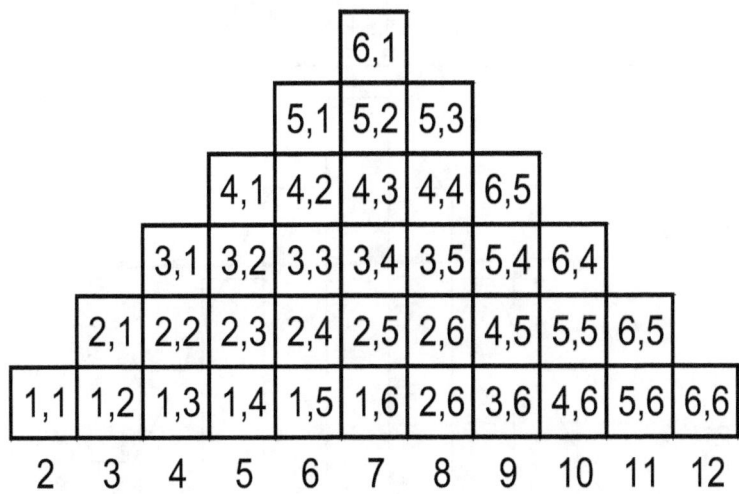

Figure 1. Block Stackup of Dice Probabilities

normal distribution. Both distributions allow calculation of an average value and a standard deviation. The lognormal is a common link in national level income values for many counties. We are interested in these because of the characteristics they have in common. Another interesting property of the standard deviation is that it allows determining how many people or other things of interest are contained within a section under the normal curve. If we take our dice example with all the numerical possibilities in each category, it would look like Figure 2.

Individuals familiar with normal distributions will recognize the curved line forms a bell shape referred to as a normal distribution curve. Notice that it peaks at the average value. There are data represented to the left and right of this peak representing the number of times, or frequency, a value or range of values occurs.

The number of standard deviations also represents a percentage of items graphed under a normal or "bell-shaped" curve. In the appendix, look up the Normal Distribution Table Starting at Mean + Z in reference to the following examples. Going from left to right in Figure 2 and upon reaching the mean, we have covered half or 50% of our data and on the chart, this is at 0.0-left column and 0.00 top left row.

To check our assumption of normally distributed data, we can tell our statistical program to perform a probability distribution

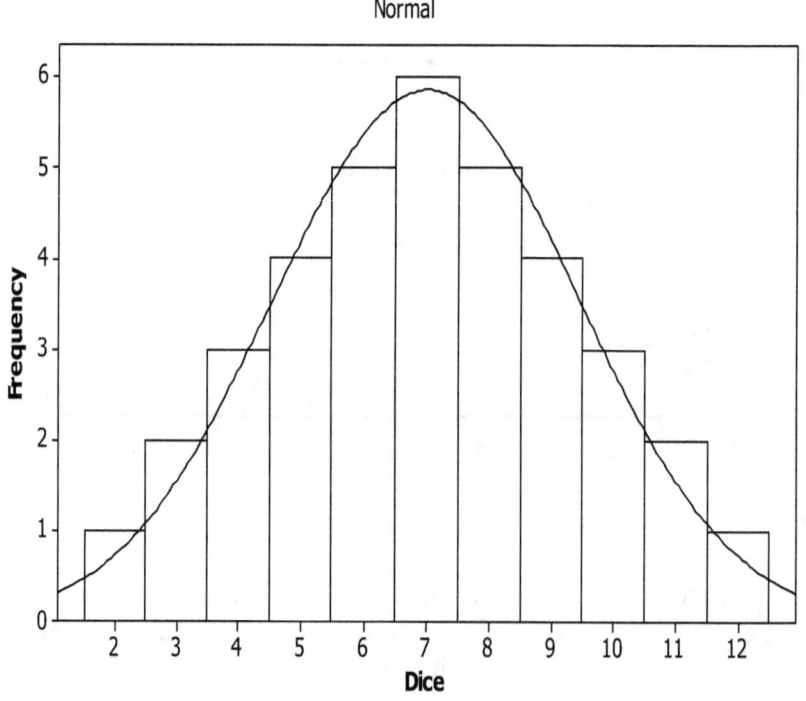

Figure 2. Histogram of Dice Number Probabilities

analysis to determine how well it fits a particular distribution. Typically, this is at the 95% confidence level. What this 95% confidence level means is that we can be 95% confident (or 95 out of

100 times) our data fits an identified distribution if our P-value is greater than .05. If our P-value is less than .05, it indicates our distribution is not likely to be a good match.

Figure 3 shows a P-value of 0.660 on our confidence interval plot for our dice data, or a strong match to a normal distribution. This is a small dataset and we can easily see each number's frequency represented by dots. In larger datasets, this is not possible due to many more numbers and overlapping values that plot over one another in the available area for individual viewing.

In the dice example, our calculated standard deviation was 2.449. This is one complete standard deviation and represents the number of units gained by traveling this much from the mean value. Going down the left side of the Normal Distribution chart to 1.0 and

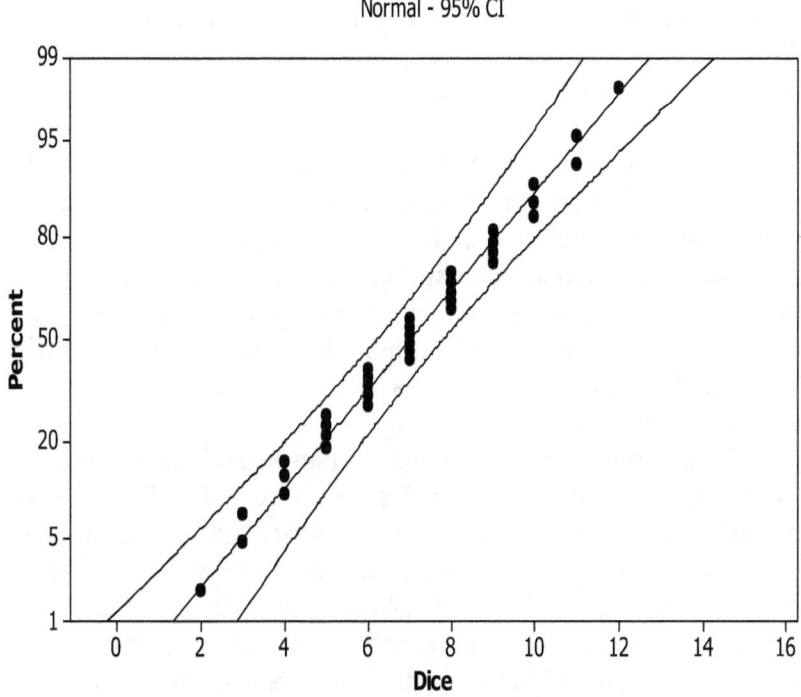

Figure 3. Confidence Interval of Dice Probabilities

over to the first column (0.00) we see that our percentage has increased from 50% to over 84% total, but to be precise, 0.8413447 – 0.5 = 0.3413447, or approximately a 34.13% increase for the first standard deviation when using rounded numbers. One standard deviation in this example represents moving 2.449 units to the right and increasing our area of coverage to 84.13% in rounded numbers, (area under the curve left of mean plus one standard deviation).

Continuing our dice example for 2 standard deviations and then three we obtain 0.9772499 or 97.72% and 0.9986501 or 99.87% in rounded numbers. Moving from our average or mean value one standard deviation moves our location from 7 to 9.449 (7+2.449) and moving to two standard deviations changes our location to 11.898 (9.449+2.449) and three standard deviations equal 14.347 or more than the possible numbers due to dataset limitations (a theoretical value). If we were to carry this out to 4.75 standard deviations this would represent a theoretical probability of one in a million or (1-0.9999990) x 1,000,000 = 1. This will become useful later in this book. In theory, the tails of a normal distribution curve extend to infinity so there is no limit on evaluating a value of interest.

Sampling

Data sampling from industries presented in this book used a methodology permitting equal representation across each occupation. Each industry contained hundreds of sampling points, varying only by the number of occupations within individual industries. To accomplish sampling of anything requires a plan. A sampling plan describes the item under investigation, what is to be measured, where measurement takes place, how measurement is achieved, and what units to report results.

The sampling plan for industries presented in this book resulted from examination and evaluation of available data sources for annual income. In this case the repository of information is the Government of the United States, Department of Labor, Bureau of Labor Statistics (BLS). The U. S. government is considered a reliable data source for research purposes and much of this information is in the public domain. The BLS gathers a wide range of data across all industry segments and compiles the information by year, in this case 2010. Universal sampling points across each industry occupation were according to BLS reported data. Measurement units are in U. S. dollars as annual income.

Many people have examined the topic of executive compensation and in doing so, they have proposed a number of theories. Each theory suffers from one or more shortcomings in that they are too general or see the subject from a single point of view. No theory describes a method for quantitatively defining where excessive compensation begins or how to determine normal compensation. When examining the subject of excessive compensation there are two camps.

The first camp does not believe excessive compensation exists. This group is comprised primarily of executives, senior managers, and groups that support these individuals in obtaining higher annual compensation in its many forms. In supporting ever-increasing requests for more and more compensation, the consultants and related groups retain their jobs for another year without giving their employer reason to fire them and look for a new group next year to feed their egos. These individuals deny the arguments of groups who propose that excessive compensation exists.

The second group believes excessive compensation exists. They point to the disparity in compensation versus the majority of workforce personnel and studies performed by various researchers that indicate no linkage to the compensation executives receive when compared to corporate performance. These proposed theories appear to identify the trees, but fail to define the forest in that the scope of view is limited.

The following chapters present a large amount of data represented in graphical figures to identify links to the national wage structure and illustrate the disparity in pay within various industries. These vary in size, from fewer than 50,000 workers to more than 9,000,000. Overall, these charts represent 30 industries and approximately 42 million workers in United States' industries for the year 2010. The lower wage boundary is set at $15,080 ($7.25 x 2080 hours/year) due to the minimum wage law.

Summary

We learned from our dice evaluation that there are 36 number combination possibilities. Ranking these possibilities by the number they represent allows us to see a frequency for each number and that they fit a normal (bell-shaped) distribution.

The normal distribution has useful properties, namely a mean or average, another number, the standard deviation (calculated value), tells us how much variation and probability or percentage of occurrence within a given number of standard deviations. We can extend the number of standard deviations out to include any number of potential possibilities for our data, even the most remote, but unlikely.

A probability plot evaluates how well our data matches a given statistical distribution and this is usually at the 95% confidence interval or, theoretically, we will be correct in our assumption of data fitting our model 95 times out of 100. The remaining 5% is referred to as the P-value and expresses as .05. Values less than .05 probably do not fit a given distribution very well and those in excess of this cutoff limit fall within the 95% probability that they do.

4 CONNECTING TO NATIONAL AND INTERNATIONAL INCOMES

     A lognormal distribution is a data set that follows a pattern described as Gibrat's Law of Proportional Effect. This is where there exists a multiplicative property of income for approximately 80% to 90% of individuals with earned income.[1,2]

     Lognormal as well as Pareto statistical distributions are appropriate for excessive compensation research due to many years of prior use in national level studies of income. A lognormal distribution originates when income data includes different occupations, varying skill levels, and medium to lower income groups. The nature of this distribution allows for ease in determining an average value, calculation of a variance, and standard deviation.[3] Another lognormal distribution attribute is its verification of applicability through usage over the decades to study national and international compensation levels for various countries. As early as 1937[4] a paper was presented during the economic conference at Oxford addressing observed income distributions fitting a logarithm for low and medium incomes and a Pareto power distribution fitting high-income values. An interesting characteristic is a breakdown of the Pareto function when moving from highly compensated to medium values of income. This is a quantifiable example of management setting up one compensation methodology for those individuals in the majority of the workforce and another for themselves.

     Having an approach that utilizes a double standard is not isolated to only management and executives within the United States.

Over the ensuing decades following presentation of this work, various researchers connected the lognormal and Pareto statistical distributions to numerous countries. One researcher noted compensation increases in the executive levels are completely out of line with individual abilities and related compensation received to the power held in a job position on a corporate organizational chart. He stated the following upon examination of compensation methods involving Western countries.

"The aggregate distribution of earning in all Western countries is approximately lognormal over most of its range, but the earnings of the top 10% to 20% of individuals follow the Pareto form, which generates a great excess of very high earnings when compared with the tail of a lognormal distribution. Individuals at the top appear to be paid according to the job they perform, rather than their ability."[5]

Therefore, higher-level positions receive compensation by job title and not by skills, training, ability, experience, and performance as in the majority of the workforce. Higher job titles on the organizational chart do not equally correspond to increased ability or productivity, but drain monetary resources because of the performance / title disconnect. Additional researchers provided results to indicate that there is significant difference between the workforce majority and those with high income. This is such that those with high income occur at a much greater rate than could be expected when examining the properties within the bulk of income distributions. Later research work reaffirmed the previous finding of income within the United States and went on to expand the finding of these distribution characteristics to Japan, India, and United Kingdom.[6] Poland and other countries have also been added to a growing list of economies with income distributions possessing lognormal and Pareto characteristics.[7]

A larger than expected result in the number of individuals with high income, when examining compensation characteristics of these distributions, leads to the conclusion that those with the power to set income levels are gaming compensation systems in their favor at the expense of investors and other stakeholders. Primary tasks and subtasks of supplying the delivery of goods and services result in a lognormal distribution, but when moving away from these primary functional operations they fall into a Pareto distribution.[8]

The above discussion covered income and compensation

within the workforce at a national level within the United States and other countries. Nevertheless, the question at this point becomes whether or not there is some type of link to national industries. One of the properties of statistical distributions is that samples taken from a population should demonstrate properties of the main distribution. Across the 30 industries represented in this book, that link is in Figure 4, which displays the lognormal link to national statistics for Forestry and Logging, and Figure 5 Paper Manufacturing Industry.

In Figure 4, the analysis of representative data shows a link to the lognormal distribution of national level analysis with a P-Value of 0.426. Figure 5 for the Paper Manufacturing Industry shows this link with a P-Value of 0.162. These industries show the lognormal link for the United States economy and present the possibility of a uniform link to lognormal distributions in other countries as well.

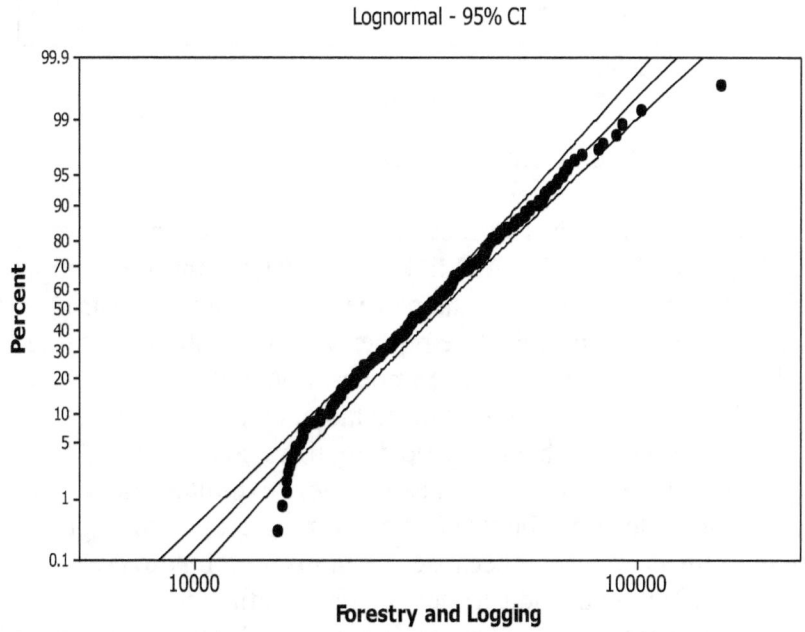

Figure 4. Forestry and Logging Lognormal Wage Analysis

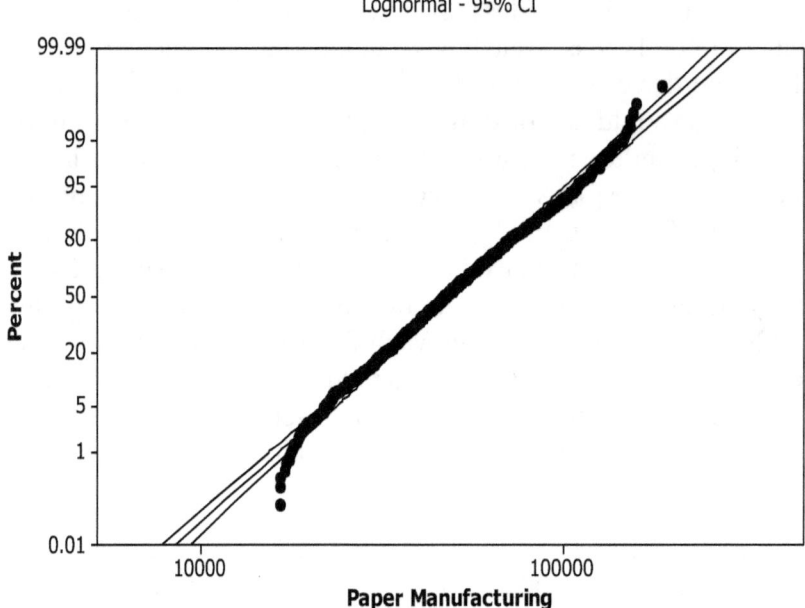

Figure 5. Paper Manufacturing Industry Lognormal Wage Analysis

Similar links to industries with economies in other countries are likely because of the inferential link to populations through samples taken within them. However, the nature of a Lognormal distribution originating from a multiplicative property of occupations, varying skill levels, and less than higher compensation will break down at some point due to a reduction in these factors within industries.

The important characteristic demonstrated by Figure 4 and Figure 5 is that national economic subsectors exhibit characteristics of international level findings when examining economic wage income. This is important because it establishes a link to create further examination of industry level data in defining excessive executive compensation by opening the door to look at international economic levels within each national economy. The following chapters present findings for 30 industry groups and a common method of analysis for defining excessive executive compensation.

5 INDUSTRIES UNDER 1,000,000 EMPLOYEES

Figure 6 shows a normal distribution curve placed over a ruler with the left limit at zero (theoretical limit of $15,080 due to minimum wage law), mean at three inches, and right limit near six inches. The second (lower scale) starts at the mean and continues to the right. The purpose is to form a uniform scale for standard deviations by placing them on consistent scale thus creating a universal way of comparing different standard deviation values across industries (size standardization). Regardless of standard deviation amount, it takes only one inch of space across the scale. Two examples (top scale): an average salary of $25,000 and $7,000 standard deviation moves from the 3-inch to 4-inch point on the ruler for a total of $32,000 and an average of $35,000 and $10,000 standard deviation moves from the 3-inch to 4-inch point for a $45,000 total. The distance is one inch for each standard deviation (universal scale); the quantity within that distance is all that changes. Figure 6's bottom scale indicates standard deviations starting at the mean and extending far beyond the illustrated normal curve into the tail. Three standard deviations from the average is representative of approximately 99.865% of the lower 80% of an industry's workforce as well as income range. Continuing to the right increases compensation received and how rare an individual becomes. A truly unique ability of 1/1,000,000 workers is represented at 4.75 standard deviations, 5.1 is 1/10,000,000, 5.6 is 1/100,000,000 and 6 is 1/1,000,000,000. If there is truly a rare executive skill, then at six standard deviations there should be less than 10 of these individuals on the planet. These factors become more interesting with discussions of distributions that follow for industries below and above 1,000,000 employees.

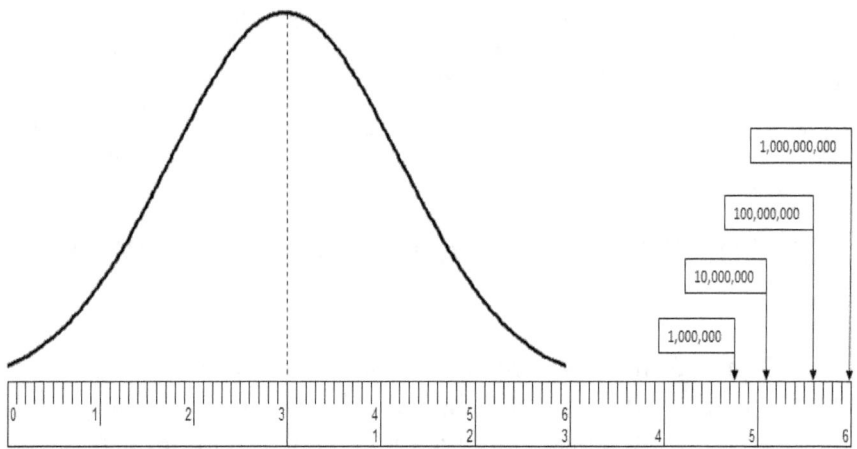

Figure 6. Standardizing Standard Deviations with a Scale

Structure of the North American Industrial Classification System (NAICS) organizes economic activities of U.S. businesses at the national level into different tiers for statistical analysis of income and other data of interest. This hierarchy follows the form of:
Super Sector Group
- Super Sector
- Sector
- Subsectors
- Industry Groups.

Twelve sectors contain the industries represented in the following two chapters within the United States that have less than 1,000,000 and more than 1,000,000 employees respectively. There are approximately 8,900,000 total employees within sectors having less than 1,000,000 employees. Individuals within these industries devoting their time to earning a living, many investing in retirement plans involving stock performance of publicly traded corporations.
The Johnson Transformation is a mathematical method to evaluate data in determining if it fits a normal statistical distribution when standard evaluation methods do not appear to. Computer

programs that apply these techniques typically generate equations that explain the data. All industry data utilized this evaluation methodology.

The bottom 80% of income data was utilized to evaluate whether or not the information fit a normal distribution. This provided a uniform methodology for each industry and follows previously discussed and established levels of evaluating national income data.

Forestry and Logging

Forestry and Logging is a part of the agriculture, forestry, fishing, and hunting sector. Industries within this area focus on the growth and harvesting of timber through management of timber tracts, forestry nurseries, amassing products related to forested areas, and logging operations. Long production cycles covering a decade or more distinguish these operations from those more traditionally associated with agricultural crop production and shorter cycle times. Many occupations comprise forestry and logging with some of the more common ones being fallers, front line supervisors and managers, equipment operators, and tractor trailer truck drivers.

Using the data within Forestry and Logging industries resulted in a histogram with a long tail to the right as displayed in Figure 7. More bars on the right side that decrease in value than on the left indicate a positively skewed distribution. There are irregular gaps in the right tail.

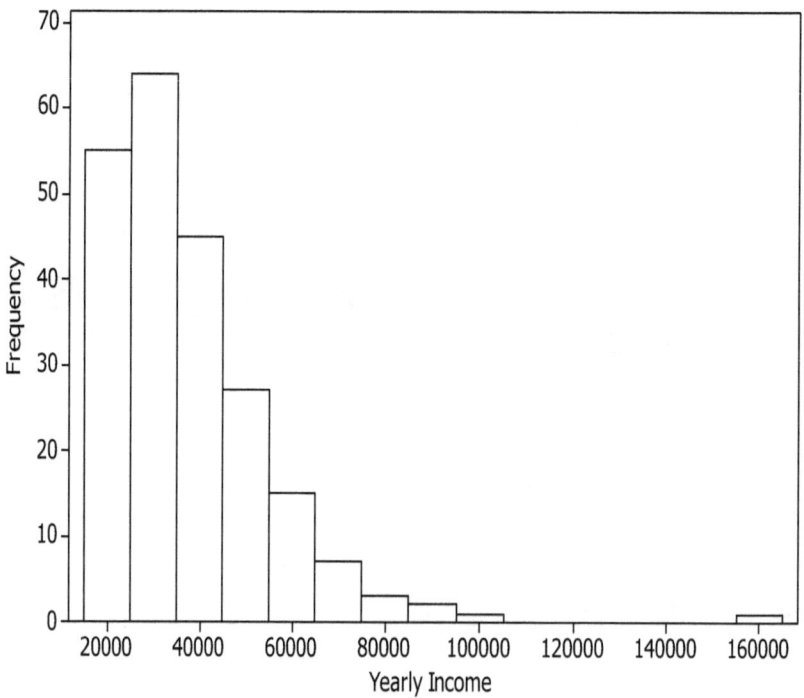

Figure 7. Forestry and Logging Wage Structure

Remember the dice example where a large number skewed the mean and standard deviation results? We can easily see there are large values in the tail of Figure 7. Using a statistical program to evaluate these values resulted in an average of $37,262 and standard deviation of $17,632. Records indicate 49,070 people earn a living in Forestry and Logging.

Removing the top 20% of data appears to eliminate these top-heavy influences and returns the data displayed in Figure 8. Average wage structure value has dropped to $30,574 with a corresponding reduction in standard deviation of $8,706. The Forestry and Logging Johnson Transformation equation is:

$$0.136541 + 0.749292 * Ln((X - 14505.1) / (48712.2 - X)).$$

Evaluating the data range of the lower 80% and the upper 20% shows the upper has more range. There appears inequitable, excessive compensation where the upper 20% of a wage structure has more range than the lower 80% of personnel. In addition, this

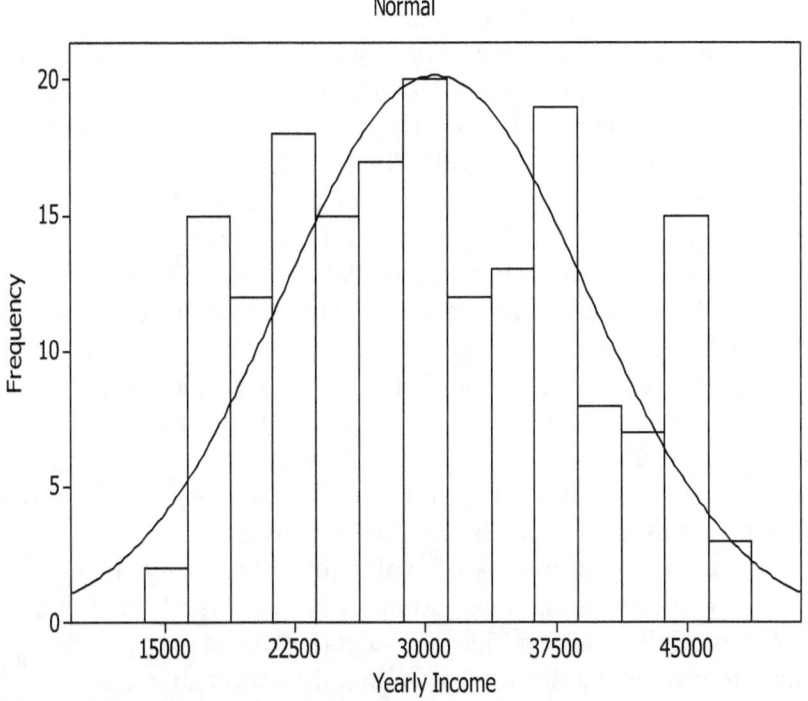

Figure 8. Forestry and Logging Normal Curve

comparison does not include the more highly paid managers and executives that exceed any of these values. Probability distribution data analysis using the Johnson Transformation results in a P-value of 0.639, confirming a good fit for a normal distribution.

Even if one were to consider Figure 7 a fair representation and the top executive (CEO) salary was limited to $1,000,000, it would require over 54 standard deviations to reach the $1,000,000 mark from this larger average: ($1,000,000 - $37,262) / $17,632 = 54.6 standard deviations (rounded).

It is easy to see from observing the charts for Forestry and Logging that each one has a different size scale for the x-axis to represent data. The statistical software automatically calculates scale size and provides an output fitting allowable space on a sheet of paper. Comparison of one figure to another in this fashion can be difficult due to scale differences. However, in an attempt to create an example that is easier to conceptualize, reconsider Figure 6. Figure 6 can be used to compare distances of the mean to any value because it places all standard deviations within a uniform distance on its scale. Regardless of standard deviation amount, it takes only one inch of space across the scale. Three standard deviations from the average represent approximately 99.865% of the lower 80% of a workforce. The further we move right, the more rare an individual becomes with a truly unique ability of 1/1,000,000 workers represented at 4.75 (inches) standard deviations. With Figure 7, the CEOs salary is over 4-1/2 <u>feet</u> away from the average.

We considered the case for all data in Figure 7 with its resulting 54 standard deviations and 4-1/2 feet distance to reach $1,000,000, let us now consider the more realistic case of Figure 8. Using the revised values of $30,574 as an average and standard deviation of $8,706, the compensation gap overruns the ruler to ($1,000,000 - $30,574) / $8,706 = 111.4 inches (rounded), or more than 9-1/4 feet to reach the hypothetical CEO's salary, much more if reality indicates salaries are larger for executives.

Another factor worthy of evaluation is the change in standard deviation values. Standard deviation for Figure 7 is $17,632 and Figure 8 is $8,706. Using Figure 7's data results in over a 50% reduction in wage variability that is directly attributable to a large range of compensation values in the right tail of this distribution: (1 - ($8,706 / $17,632)) * 100 = 50.6% (rounded).

Oil and Gas Extraction

Oil and gas extraction is an industry group within the mining, quarrying, and oil and gas extraction sector. Operations include crude petroleum and natural gas exploration, all stages of well development, and preparation of product up to shipping operations from the property where it is produced. There are many occupations enabling oil and gas to be productive and include geoscientists, roustabouts, and wellhead pumpers.

Using the data within the Oil and Gas Extraction industries resulted in a histogram with a long tail to the right as displayed in Figure 9. More bars on the right side that decrease in value than on the left indicate a positively skewed distribution. There are irregular gaps in the right tail.

Remember the dice example where a large number skewed the mean and standard deviation results? We can easily see there are large values in the tail of Figure 9. Using a statistical program to evaluate all data resulted in an average of $67,658 and standard

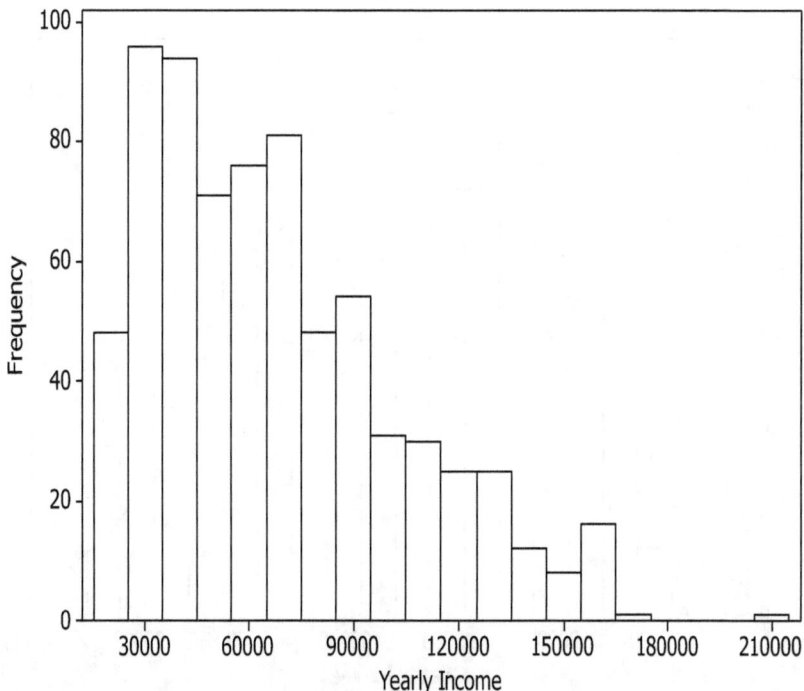

Figure 9. Oil and Gas Extraction Wage Structure

deviation of $35,708. Records indicate 154,980 people earn a living in Oil and Gas Extraction.

Removing the top 20% of data appears to eliminate these top-heavy influences and returns the data displayed in Figure 10. Average wage structure value has dropped to $53,388 with a corresponding reduction in standard deviation of $21,538. The Oil and Gas Extraction Johnson Transformation equation is:

$$0.200709 + 0.749847 * Ln((X - 14326.3) / (101958 - X)).$$

Evaluating the data range of the lower 80% and the upper 20% shows the upper has more range. There appears inequitable, excessive compensation where the upper 20% of a wage structure has more range than the lower 80% of personnel. In addition, this comparison does not include the more highly paid managers and executives that exceed any of these values. Probability distribution data analysis using the Johnson Transformation results in a P-value of 0.409, confirming a good fit for a normal distribution.

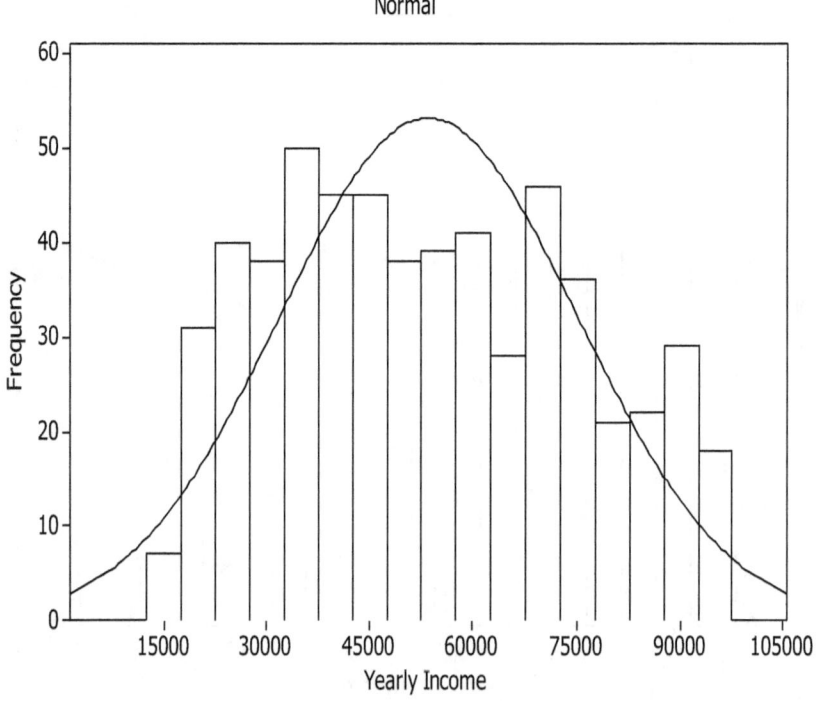

Figure 10. Oil and Gas Extraction Normal Curve

Even if one were to consider Figure 9 a fair representation and the top executive (CEO) salary was limited to $1,000,000, it would require over 26 standard deviations to reach the $1,000,000 mark from this larger average: ($1,000,000 - $67,658) / $35,706 = 26.1 standard deviations (rounded).

It is easy to see from observing the charts for Oil and Gas Extraction that each one has a different size scale for the x-axis to represent data. The statistical software automatically calculates scale size and provides an output fitting allowable space on a sheet of paper. Comparison of one figure to another in this fashion can be difficult due to scale differences. However, in an attempt to create an example that is easier to conceptualize, reconsider Figure 6. Figure 6 can be used to compare distances of the mean to any value because it places all standard deviations within a uniform distance on its scale. Regardless of standard deviation amount, it takes only one inch of space across the scale. Three standard deviations from the average represent approximately 99.865% of the lower 80% of a workforce. The further we move right, the more rare an individual becomes with a truly unique ability of 1/1,000,000 workers represented at 4.75 (inches) standard deviations. With Figure 9, the CEOs salary is over 2 <u>feet</u> away from the average.

We considered the case for all data in Figure 9 with its resulting 26 standard deviations and 2 feet distance to reach $1,000,000, let us now consider the more realistic case of Figure 10. Using the revised values of $53,388 as an average and standard deviation of $21,538, the compensation gap overruns the ruler to ($1,000,000 - $53,388) / $21,538 = 44 inches (rounded), or more than 3-2/3 feet to reach the hypothetical CEO's salary, much more if reality indicates salaries are larger for executives.

Another factor worthy of evaluation is the change in standard deviation values. Standard deviation for Figure 9 is $35,706 and Figure 10 is $21,588. Using Figure 10's data results in over a 40% reduction in wage variability that is directly attributable to a large range of compensation values in the right tail of this distribution: (1 - ($21,538 / $35,706)) * 100 = 40% (rounded).

Heavy and Civil Engineering Construction

This industry group is part of the larger construction sector. Principle involvement includes A-Z construction of engineering projects such as highways, bridges, and dams for hydroelectric power and flood control. Specialty trade contractors may fabricate specific components or subsystems for these projects. These activities are not normally associated with building construction. Work on these structures can range from new construction to additions, alterations, maintenance functions, and repairs. Among the more common occupations are heavy equipment operators, engineers, tractor trailer drivers, carpenters, and various laborers.

Using the data within the Heavy and Civil Engineering Construction industries resulted in a histogram with a long tail to the right as displayed in Figure 11. More bars on the right side that decrease in value than on the left indicate a positively skewed distribution. There are irregular gaps in the right tail.

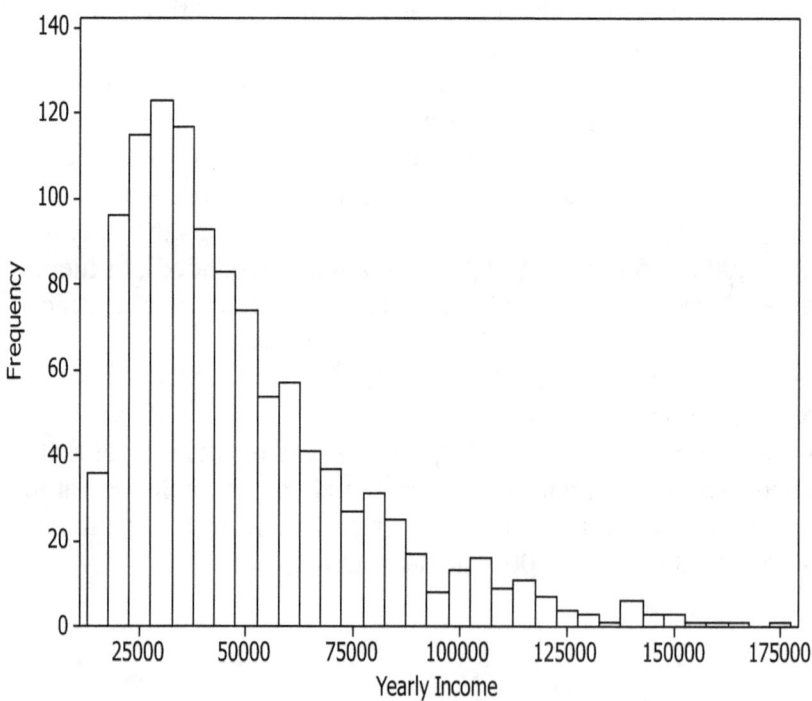

Figure 11. Heavy and Civil Engineering Wage Structure

Remember the dice example where a large number skewed the mean and standard deviation results? We can easily see there are large values in the tail of Figure 11. Using a statistical program to evaluate all data resulted in an average of $48,719 and standard deviation of $27,356. Records indicate 840,680 people earn a living in Heavy and Civil Engineering Construction.

Removing the top 20% of data appears to eliminate these top-heavy influences and returns the data in Figure 12. Average wage structure value has dropped to $37,567 with a corresponding reduction in standard deviation of $13,669. The Heavy and Civil Engineering Construction Johnson Transformation equation is:

$$0.365982 + 0.821877 * Ln((X - 13777.4) / (71670.1 - X)).$$

Evaluating the data range of the lower 80% and the upper 20% shows the upper has more range. There appears inequitable, excessive compensation where the upper 20% of a wage structure has more range than the lower 80% of personnel. In addition, this

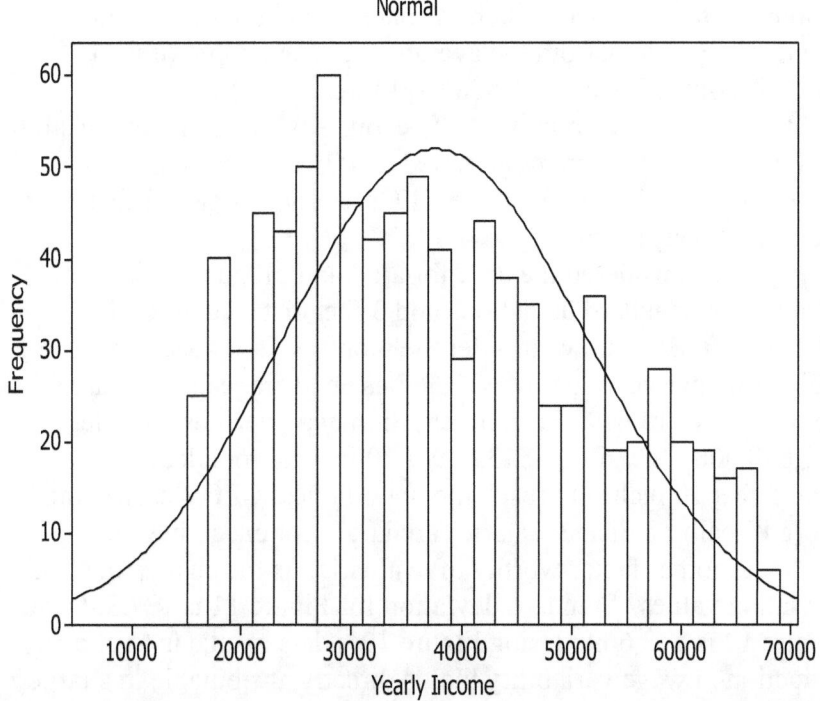

Figure 12. Heavy and Civil Engineering Construction Normal Curve

comparison does not include the more highly paid managers and executives that exceed any of these values. Probability distribution data analysis using the Johnson Transformation results in a P-value of 0.855, confirming a good fit for a normal distribution.

Even if one were to consider Figure 11 a fair representation and the top executive (CEO) salary was limited to $1,000,000, it would require over 34 standard deviations to reach the $1,000,000 mark from this larger average: ($1,000,000 - $48,719) / $27,356 = 34.8 standard deviations (rounded).

It is easy to see from observing the charts for Heavy and Civil Engineering Construction that each one has a different size scale for the x-axis to represent data. The statistical software automatically calculates scale size and provides an output fitting allowable space on a sheet of paper. Comparison of one figure to another in this fashion can be difficult due to scale differences. However, in an attempt to create an example that is easier to conceptualize, reconsider Figure 6. Figure 6 can be used to compare distances of the mean to any value because it places all standard deviations within a uniform distance on its scale. Regardless of standard deviation amount, it takes only one inch of space across the scale. Three standard deviations from the average represent approximately 99.865% of the lower 80% of a workforce. The further we move right, the more rare an individual becomes with a truly unique ability of 1/1,000,000 workers represented at 4.75 (inches) standard deviations. With Figure 12, the CEOs salary is almost 3 <u>feet</u> away from the average.

We considered the case for all data in Figure 11 with its resulting 34 standard deviations and 3 feet distance to reach $1,000,000, let us now consider the more realistic case of Figure 12. Using the revised values of $37,567 as an average and standard deviation of $13,669, the compensation gap overruns the ruler to ($1,000,000 - $37,657) / $13,669 = 70 inches (rounded), or more than 5 feet 10 inches to reach the hypothetical CEO's salary, much more if reality indicates salaries are larger for executives.

Another factor worthy of evaluation is the change in standard deviation values. Standard deviation for Figure 11 is $27,356 and Figure 12 is $13,669. Using Figure 12's data results in over a 50% reduction in wage variability that is directly attributable to a large range of compensation values in the right tail of this distribution: (1 - ($13,669 / $27,356)) * 100 = 50% (rounded).

Wood Product Manufacturing

This industry group is part of the manufacturing sector involving creation of lumber, wood containers, wood flooring products, building trusses, manufactured homes, and prefabricated wooden buildings, among others. Typical processes involve sawing, shaping, assembling, planning, and lamination. Cabinetmakers, carpenters, machine setters, supervisors and managers, assemblers, and off bearers are common occupations.

Using the data within the Wood Product Manufacturing industries resulted in a histogram with a long tail to the right as displayed in Figure 13. More bars on the right side that decrease in value than on the left indicate a positively skewed distribution. There are irregular gaps in the right tail.

Remember the dice example where a large number skewed the mean and standard deviation results? We can easily see there are large values in the tail of Figure 13. Using a statistical program to evaluate all data resulted in an average of $42,560 and standard

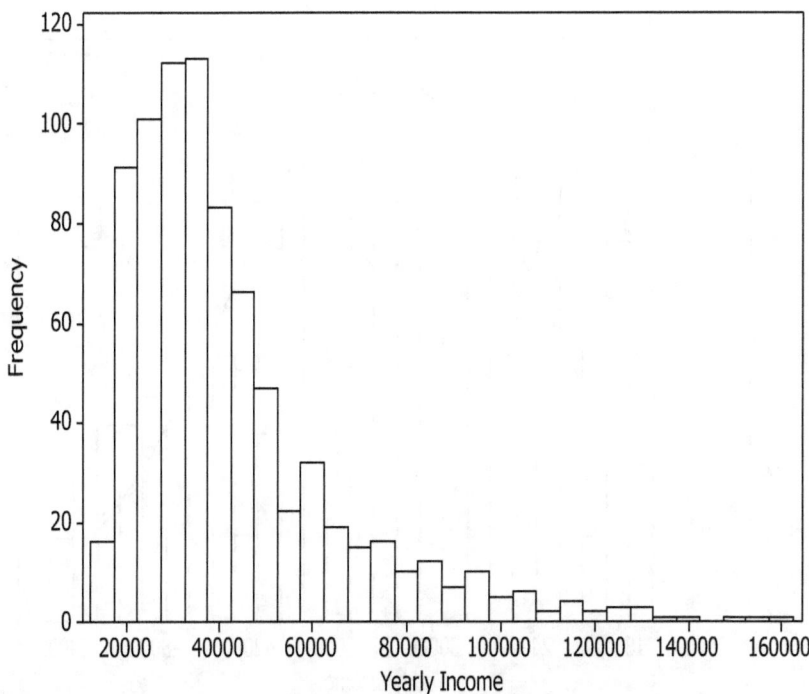

Figure 13. Wood Product Manufacturing Wage Structure

deviation of $23,227. Records indicate 345,110 people earn a living in Wood Product Manufacturing.

Removing the top 20% of data appears to eliminate these top-heavy influences and returns the data displayed in Figure 14. Average wage structure value has dropped to $33,082 with a corresponding reduction in standard deviation of $9,804. The Wood Product Manufacturing Johnson Transformation equation is:

$$0.366976 + 0.816675 * Ln((X - 14916.7) / (66932.7 - X))$$

Evaluating the data range of the lower 80% and the upper 20% shows the upper has more range. There appears inequitable, excessive compensation where the upper 20% of a wage structure has more range than the lower 80% of personnel. In addition, this comparison does not include the more highly paid managers and executives that exceed any of these values. Probability distribution data analysis using the Johnson Transformation results in a P-value of 0.414, confirming a good fit for a normal distribution.

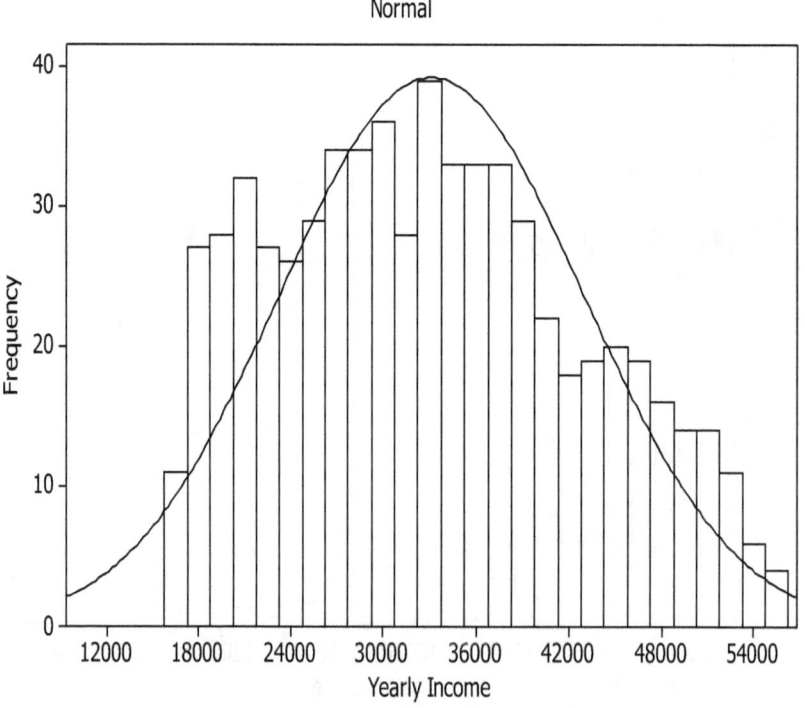

Figure 14. Wood Product Manufacturing Normal Curve

Even if one were to consider Figure 14 a fair representation and the top executive (CEO) salary was limited to $1,000,000, it would require over 41 standard deviations to reach the $1,000,000 mark from this larger average: ($1,000,000 - $42,560) / $23,227 = 41.2 standard deviations (rounded).

It is easy to see from observing the charts for Wood Product Manufacturing that each one has a different size scale for the x-axis to represent data. The statistical software automatically calculates scale size and provides an output fitting allowable space on a sheet of paper. Comparison of one figure to another in this fashion can be difficult due to scale differences. However, in an attempt to create an example that is easier to conceptualize, reconsider Figure 6. Figure 6 can be used to compare distances of the mean to any value because it places all standard deviations within a uniform distance on its scale. Regardless of standard deviation amount, it takes only one inch of space across the scale. Three standard deviations from the average represent approximately 99.865% of the lower 80% of a workforce. The further we move right, the more rare an individual becomes with a truly unique ability of 1/1,000,000 workers represented at 4.75 (inches) standard deviations. With Figure 13, the CEOs salary is over 3 <u>feet</u> away from the average.

We considered the case for all data in Figure 13 with its resulting 41 standard deviations and 3 feet distance to reach $1,000,000, let us now consider the more realistic case of Figure 14. Using the revised values of $33,082 as an average and standard deviation of $9,804, the compensation gap overruns the ruler to ($1,000,000 - $33,082) / $9,804 = 98.6 inches (rounded), or more than 8 feet 2 inches to reach the hypothetical CEO's salary, much more if reality indicates salaries are larger for executives.

Another factor worthy of evaluation is the change in standard deviation values. Standard deviation for Figure 13 is $23,227 and Figure 14 is $9,804. Using Figure 14's data results in over a 57% reduction in wage variability that is directly attributable to a large range of compensation values in the right tail of this distribution: (1 - ($9,804 / $23,227)) * 100 = 57.8% (rounded).

Paper Manufacturing

Paper manufacturing is another industry group of manufacturing and involves creation of pulp, paper and products related to the conversion of paper. These processes involve segregating cellulose fiber from wood impurities, matting the fiber into sheets, and creating a range of products from cutting, shaping, coating, and laminating. There are many occupations within this industry, among them are machine setters and operators, front line supervisors and managers, personnel who operate industrial trucks and tractors, and printing machine operators.

Using the data within the Paper Manufacturing industries resulted in a histogram with a long tail to the right as displayed in Figure 15. More bars on the right side that decrease in value than on the left indicate a positively skewed distribution. There are irregular gaps in the right tail.

Remember the dice example where a large number skewed the mean and standard deviation results? We can easily see there are

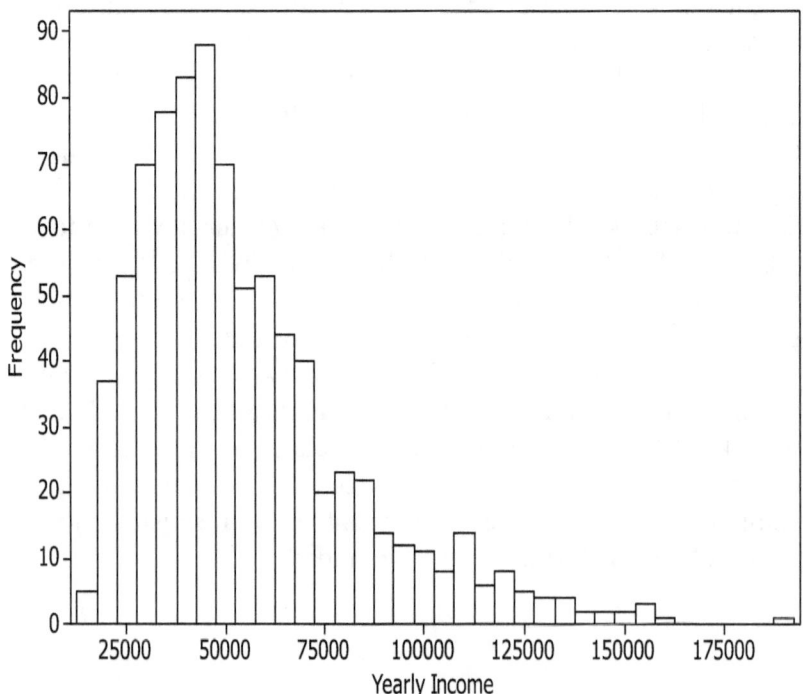

Figure 15. Paper Manufacturing Wage Structure

large values in the tail of Figure 15. Using a statistical program to evaluate all data resulted in an average of $54,600 and standard deviation of $27,146. Records indicate 393,540 people earn a living in Paper Manufacturing.

Removing the top 20% of data appears to eliminate these top-heavy influences and returns the data displayed in Figure 16. Average wage structure value has dropped to $43,630 with a corresponding reduction in standard deviation of $14,002. The Paper Manufacturing Johnson Transformation equation is:

$$0.366976 + 0.816675 * Ln((X - 14916.7) / (66932.7 - X))$$

Evaluating the data range of the lower 80% and the upper 20% shows the upper has more range. There appears inequitable, excessive compensation where the upper 20% of a wage structure has more range than the lower 80% of personnel. In addition, this comparison does not include the more highly paid managers and executives that exceed any of these values. Probability distribution

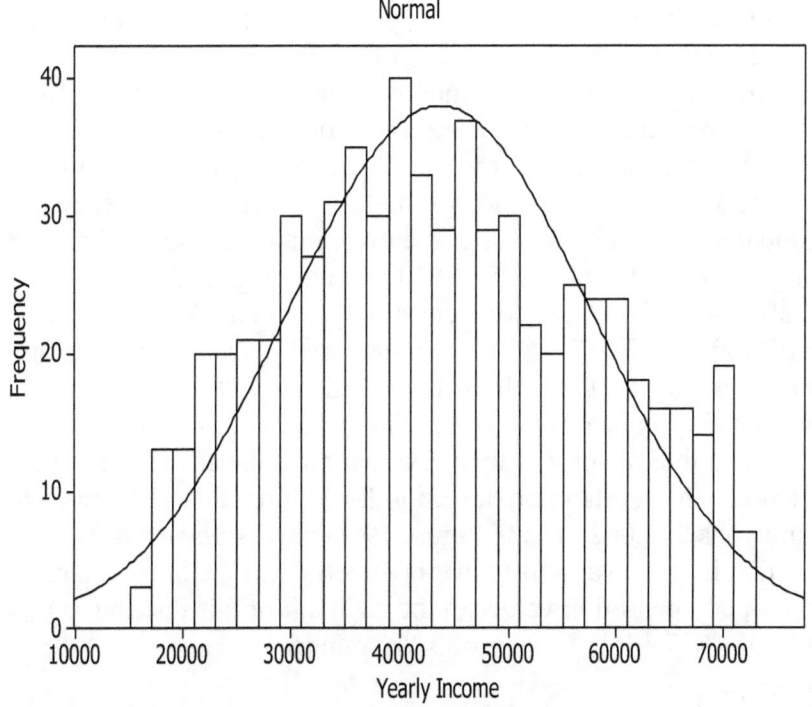

Figure 16. Paper Manufacturing Normal Curve

data analysis using the Johnson Transformation results in a P-value of 0.188, confirming a good fit for a normal distribution.

Even if one were to consider Figure 15 a fair representation and the top executive (CEO) salary was limited to $1,000,000, it would require over 34 standard deviations to reach the $1,000,000 mark from this larger average: ($1,000,000 - $54,600) / $27,146 = 34.8 standard deviations (rounded).

It is easy to see from observing the charts for Paper Manufacturing that each one has a different size scale for the x-axis to represent data. The statistical software automatically calculates scale size and provides an output fitting allowable space on a sheet of paper. Comparison of one figure to another in this fashion can be difficult due to scale differences. However, in an attempt to create an example that is easier to conceptualize, reconsider Figure 6. Figure 6 can be used to compare distances of the mean to any value because it places all standard deviations within a uniform distance on its scale. Regardless of standard deviation amount, it takes only one inch of space across the scale. Three standard deviations from the average represent approximately 99.865% of the lower 80% of a workforce. The further we move right, the more rare an individual becomes with a truly unique ability of 1/1,000,000 workers represented at 4.75 (inches) standard deviations. With Figure 15, the CEOs salary is almost 3 <u>feet</u> away from the average.

We considered the case for all data in Figure 15 with its resulting 34 standard deviations and almost 3 feet distance to reach $1,000,000, let us now consider the more realistic case of Figure 16. Using the revised values of $43,630 as an average and standard deviation of $14,002, the compensation gap overruns the ruler to ($1,000,000 - $43,630) / $14,002 = 68.3 inches (rounded), or more than 5 feet 8 inches to reach the hypothetical CEO's salary, much more if reality indicates salaries are larger for executives.

Another factor worthy of evaluation is the change in standard deviation values. Standard deviation for Figure 15 is $27,146 and Figure 16 is $14,002. Using Figure 19's data results in a 48% reduction in wage variability that is directly attributable to a large range of compensation values in the right tail of this distribution: (1 - ($14,002 / $27,146)) * 100 = 48.4% (rounded).

Chemical Manufacturing

The manufacturing sector has a number of industry groups, among them is Chemical Manufacturing. Focus in this area involves changing organic and inorganic materials through chemical processes and creation of new products from the output. Typical products include resins, synthetic rubber, synthetic fibers and filaments, pharmaceuticals, paints, adhesives, soap and other cleaning compounds. Chemists, equipment operators, and operation of packaging and filling equipment are frequent occupations.

Using the data within the Chemical Manufacturing industries resulted in a histogram with a long tail to the right as displayed in Figure 17. More bars on the right side that decrease in value than on the left indicate a positively skewed distribution. There are irregular gaps in the right tail.

Remember the dice example where a large number skewed the mean and standard deviation results? We can easily see there are large values in the tail of Figure 17. Using a statistical program to

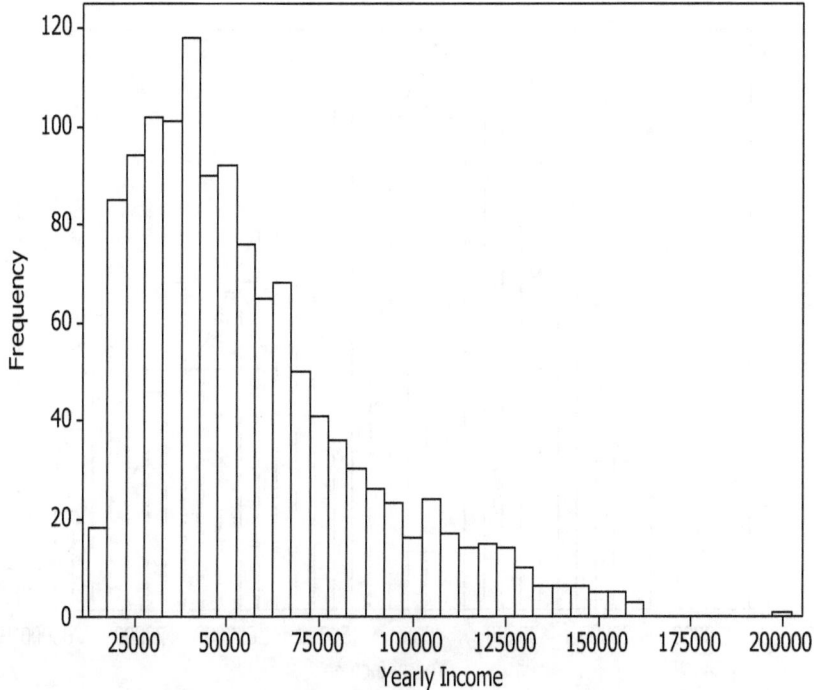

Figure 17. Chemical Manufacturing Wage Structure

evaluate all data resulted in an average of $56,009 and standard deviation of $30,528. Records indicate 792,830 people earn a living in Chemical Manufacturing.

Removing the top 20% of data appears to eliminate these top-heavy influences and returns the data displayed in Figure 23. Average wage structure value has dropped to $43,600 with a corresponding reduction in standard deviation of $16,232. The Chemical Manufacturing Johnson Transformation equation is:

$$0.366976 + 0.816675 * Ln((X - 14916.7) / (66932.7 - X)).$$

In addition, this comparison does not include the more highly paid managers and executives that exceed any of these values. Probability distribution data analysis using the Johnson Transformation results in a P-value of 0.599, confirming a good fit for a normal distribution.

Even if one were to consider Figure 17 a fair representation

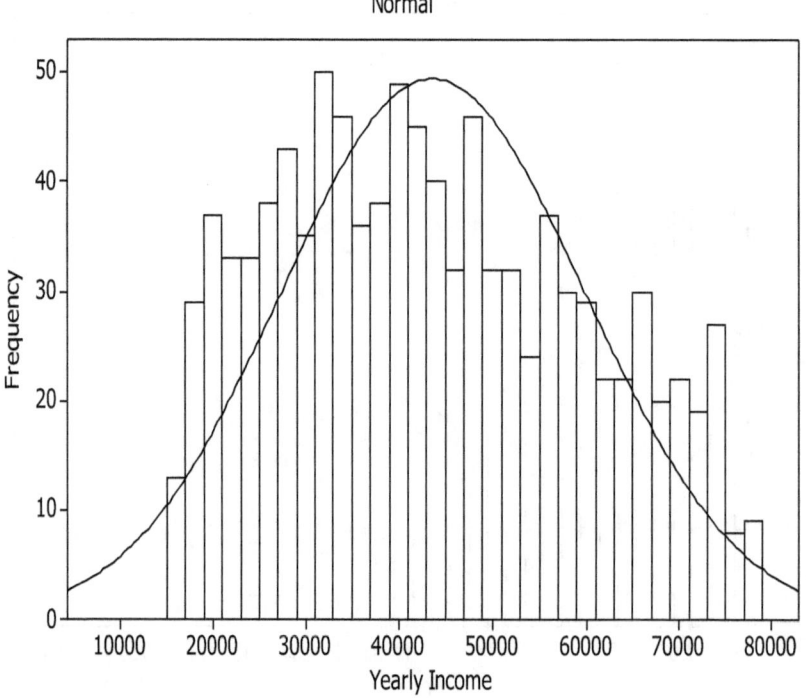

Figure 18. Chemical Manufacturing Normal Curve

and the top executive (CEO) salary was limited to $1,000,000, it would require over 30 standard deviations to reach the $1,000,000 mark from this larger industry average: ($1,000,000 - $56,009) / $30,528 = 30.9 standard deviations (rounded).

It is easy to see from observing the charts for Chemical Manufacturing that each one has a different size scale for the x-axis to represent data. The statistical software automatically calculates scale size and provides an output fitting allowable space on a sheet of paper. Comparison of one figure to another in this fashion can be difficult due to scale differences. However, in an attempt to create an example that is easier to conceptualize, reconsider Figure 6. Figure 6 can be used to compare distances of the mean to any value because it places all standard deviations within a uniform distance on its scale. Regardless of standard deviation amount, it takes only one inch of space across the scale. Three standard deviations from the average represent approximately 99.865% of the lower 80% of a workforce. The further we move right, the more rare an individual becomes with a truly unique ability of 1/1,000,000 workers represented at 4.75 (inches) standard deviations. With Figure 17, the CEOs salary is over 2-1/2 _feet_ away from the average.

We considered the case for all data in Figure 17 with its resulting 30.9 standard deviations and 2-1/2 feet distance to reach $1,000,000, let us now consider the more realistic case of Figure 18. Using the revised values of $40,600 as an average and standard deviation of $16,232, the compensation gap overruns the ruler to ($1,000,000 - $43,600) / $16,232 = 58.9 inches (rounded), or almost 5 feet to reach the hypothetical CEO's salary, much more if reality indicates salaries are larger for executives.

Another factor worthy of evaluation is the change in standard deviation values. Standard deviation for Figure 17 is $30,528 and Figure 18 is $16,232. Using Figure 18's data results in over a 46% reduction in wage variability that is directly attributable to a large range of compensation values in the right tail of this distribution: (1 - ($16,232 / $30,528)) * 100 = 46.8% (rounded).

Plastics and Rubber Products Manufacturing

As the name sounds, the Plastics and Rubber Products Manufacturing industries creates products through processing plastic and rubber materials. Plastics are increasingly employed as an alternative for rubber based products and industries tend to focus on one or the other. A variety of personnel performing duties as machine setters, extruding and forming operators, testers, packaging operators, and supervisors and managers are common occupations.

Using the data within the Plastics and Rubber Products Manufacturing industries resulted in a histogram with a long tail to the right as displayed in Figure 19. More bars on the right side that decrease in value than on the left indicate a positively skewed distribution. There are irregular gaps in the right tail.

Remember the dice example where a large number skewed the mean and standard deviation results? We can easily see there are large values in the tail of Figure 19. Using a statistical program to evaluate all data resulted in an average of $47,359 and standard

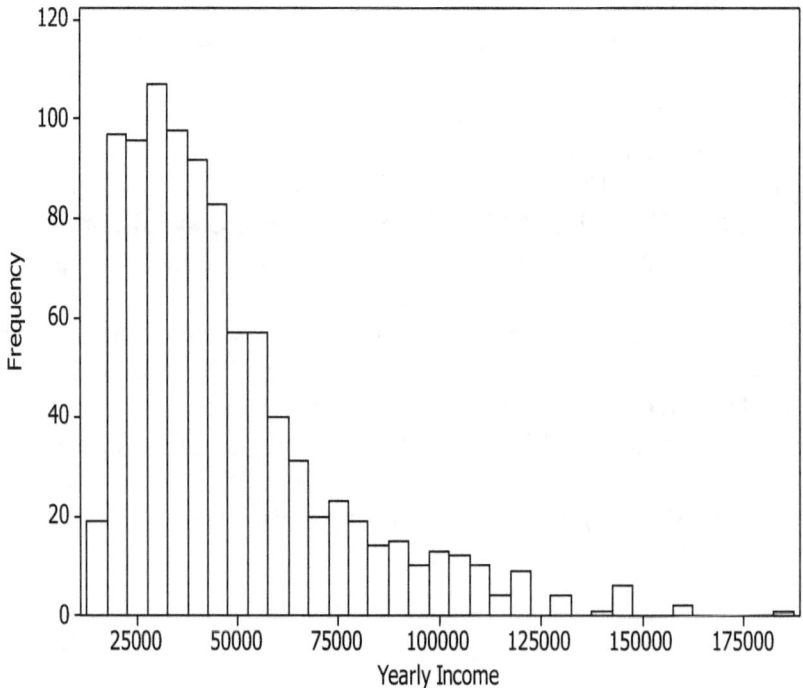

Figure 19. Plastics and Rubber Products Wage Structure

deviation of $26,153. Records indicate 625,000 people earn a living in Plastics and Rubber Products.

Removing the top 20% of data appears to eliminate these top-heavy influences and returns the data displayed in Figure 20. Average wage structure value has dropped to $36,651 with a corresponding reduction in standard deviation of $12,422. The Plastics and Rubber Products Johnson Transformation equation is:

$$0.366976 + 0.816675 * Ln((X - 14916.7) / (66932.7 - X))$$

Evaluating the data range of the lower 80% and the upper 20% shows the upper has more range. There appears inequitable, excessive compensation where the upper 20% of a wage structure has more range than the lower 80% of personnel. In addition, this comparison does not include the more highly paid managers and executives that exceed any of these values. Probability distribution data analysis using the Johnson Transformation results in a P-value of 0.235, confirming a good fit for a normal distribution.

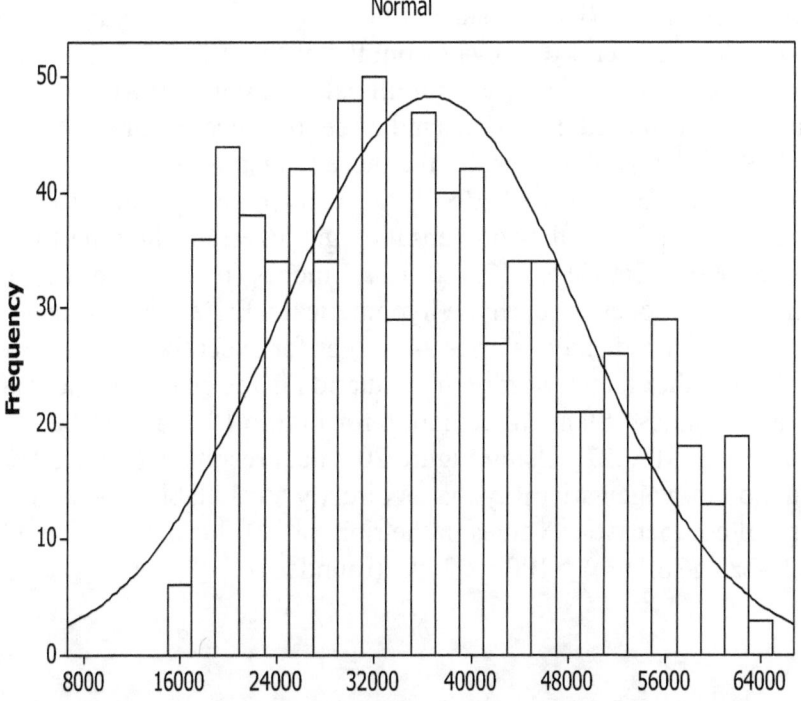

Figure 20. Plastics and Rubber Products Normal Curve

Even if one were to consider Figure 19 a fair representation and the top executive (CEO) salary was limited to $1,000,000, it would require over 36 standard deviations to reach the $1,000,000 mark from this larger average: ($1,000,000 - $47,359) / $26,153 = 36.4 standard deviations (rounded).

It is easy to see from observing the charts for Plastics and Rubber Products that each one has a different size scale for the x-axis to represent data. The statistical software automatically calculates scale size and provides an output fitting allowable space on a sheet of paper. Comparison of one figure to another in this fashion can be difficult due to scale differences. However, in an attempt to create an example that is easier to conceptualize, reconsider Figure 6. Figure 6 can be used to compare distances of the mean to any value because it places all standard deviations within a uniform distance on its scale. Regardless of standard deviation amount, it takes only one inch of space across the scale. Three standard deviations from the average represent approximately 99.865% of the lower 80% of a workforce. The further we move right, the more rare an individual becomes with a truly unique ability of 1/1,000,000 workers represented at 4.75 (inches) standard deviations. With Figure 19, the CEOs salary is over 3 <u>feet</u> away from the average.

We considered the case for all data in Figure 19 with its resulting 36 standard deviations and 3 feet distance to reach $1,000,000, let us now consider the more realistic case of Figure 20. Using the revised values of $36,651 as an average and standard deviation of $12,422, the compensation gap overruns the ruler to ($1,000,000 - $36,651) / $12,422 = 77.5 inches (rounded), or more than 6 feet 5 inches to reach the hypothetical CEO's salary, much more if reality indicates salaries are larger for executives.

Another factor worthy of evaluation is the change in standard deviation values. Standard deviation for Figure 19 is $26,153 and Figure 20 is $12,422. Using Figure 20's data results in over a 52% reduction in wage variability that is directly attributable to a large range of compensation values in the right tail of this distribution: (1 - ($12,422 / $26,153)) * 100 = 52.4% (rounded).

Machinery Manufacturing

These industries create products that apply mechanical force through gears, levers, and hydraulics for a wide variety of applications. Many processes are involved in the creation of these devices: forging, bending, machining, punching, and so on. Multiple operations and processes are common in achieving an end result. Assemblers, engineers, tool and die makers, welders, CAD designers, etc. are common occupations.

Using the data within the Machinery Manufacturing industries resulted in a histogram with a long tail to the right as displayed in Figure 21. More bars on the right side that decrease in value than on the left indicate a positively skewed distribution. There are irregular gaps in the right tail.

Remember the dice example where a large number skewed the mean and standard deviation results? We can easily see there are large values in the tail of Figure 21. Using a statistical program to evaluate all data resulted in an average of $51,089 and standard

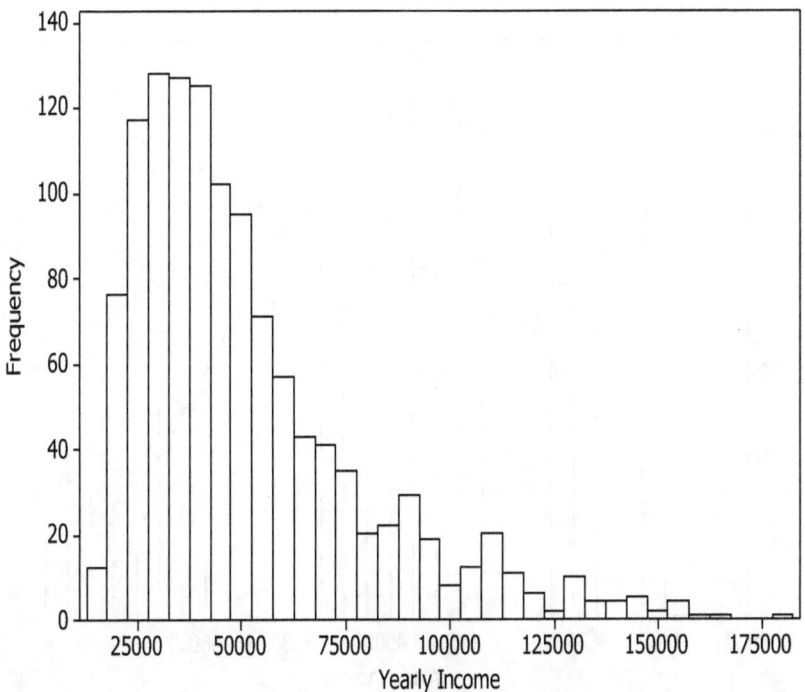

Figure 21. Machinery Manufacturing Wage Structure

deviation of $27,536. Records indicate 980,900 people earn a living in Machinery Manufacturing.

Removing the top 20% of data appears to eliminate these top-heavy influences and returns the data displayed in Figure 22. Average wage structure value has dropped to $39,751 with a corresponding reduction in standard deviation of $13,150. The Machinery Manufacturing Johnson Transformation equation is:

$$0.503715 + 0.952512 * Ln((X - 14273.2) / (64194.6 - X)).$$

Evaluating the data range of the lower 80% and the upper 20% shows the upper has more range. There appears inequitable, excessive compensation where the upper 20% of a wage structure has more range than the lower 80% of personnel. In addition, this comparison does not include the more highly paid managers and executives that exceed any of these values. Probability distribution data analysis using the Johnson Transformation results in a P-value of 0.737, confirming a good fit for a normal distribution.

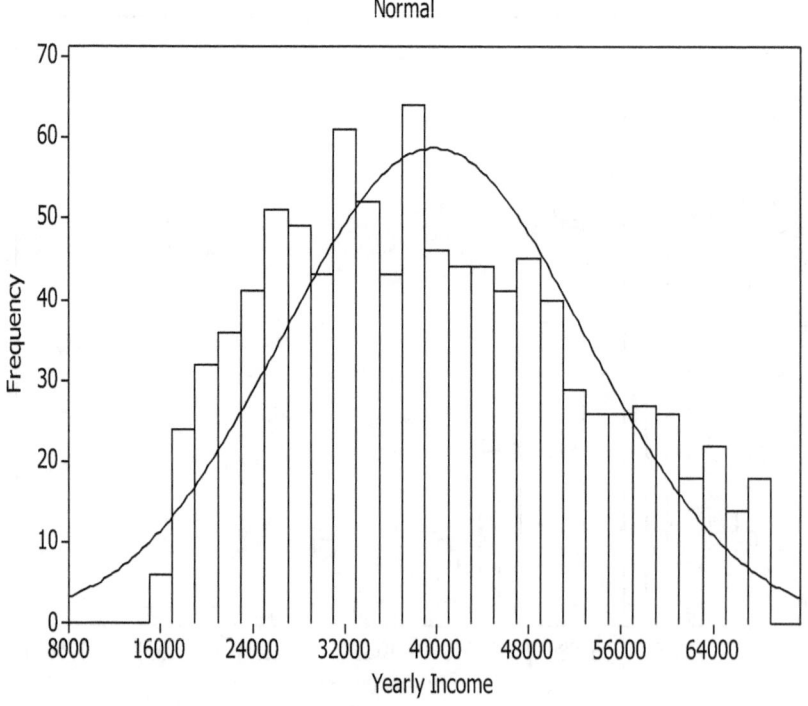

Figure 22. Machinery Manufacturing Normal Curve

Even if one were to consider Figure 21 a fair representation and the top executive (CEO) salary was limited to $1,000,000, it would require over 34 standard deviations to reach the $1,000,000 mark from this larger average: ($1,000,000 - $51,089) / $27,536 = 34.5 standard deviations (rounded).

It is easy to see from observing the charts for Machinery Manufacturing that each one has a different size scale for the x-axis to represent data. The statistical software automatically calculates scale size and provides an output fitting allowable space on a sheet of paper. Comparison of one figure to another in this fashion can be difficult due to scale differences. However, in an attempt to create an example that is easier to conceptualize, reconsider Figure 6. Figure 6 can be used to compare distances of the mean to any value because it places all standard deviations within a uniform distance on its scale. Regardless of standard deviation amount, it takes only one inch of space across the scale. Three standard deviations from the average represent approximately 99.865% of the lower 80% of a workforce. The further we move right, the more rare an individual becomes with a truly unique ability of 1/1,000,000 workers represented at 4.75 (inches) standard deviations. With Figure 21, the CEOs salary is almost 3 <u>feet</u> away from the average.

We considered the case for all data in Figure 21 with its resulting 34 standard deviations and almost 3 feet distance to reach $1,000,000, let us now consider the more realistic case of Figure 22. Using the revised values of $39,751 as an average and standard deviation of $13,150, the compensation gap overruns the ruler to ($1,000,000 - $39,751) / $13,150 = 73.0 inches (rounded), or more than 6 feet to reach the hypothetical CEO's salary, much more if reality indicates salaries are larger for executives.

Another factor worthy of evaluation is the change in standard deviation values. Standard deviation for Figure 21 is $27,536 and Figure 22 is $13,150. Using Figure 22's data results in over a 52% reduction in wage variability that is directly attributable to a large range of compensation values in the right tail of this distribution: (1 - ($13,150 / $27,536)) * 100 = 52.2% (rounded).

Electrical Equipment, Appliance, and Component Manufacturing

Industries within the EEACM are involved with creating products for electrical power generation, distribution, and usage. A wide range of products fall within this area: bulbs, fixtures, appliances of all sizes, transformers and switchgear equipment name a few. The storage of electrical power in batteries, wiring, and components are included. Inspectors, supervisors, managers, and machine operators are common occupations.

Using the data within the EEACM group resulted in a histogram with a long tail to the right as displayed in Figure 23. More bars on the right side that decrease in value than on the left indicate a positively skewed distribution. There are irregular gaps in the right tail.

Remember the dice example where a large number skewed the mean and standard deviation results? We can easily see there are large values in the tail of Figure 23. Using a statistical program to evaluate all data resulted in an average of $52,671 and standard

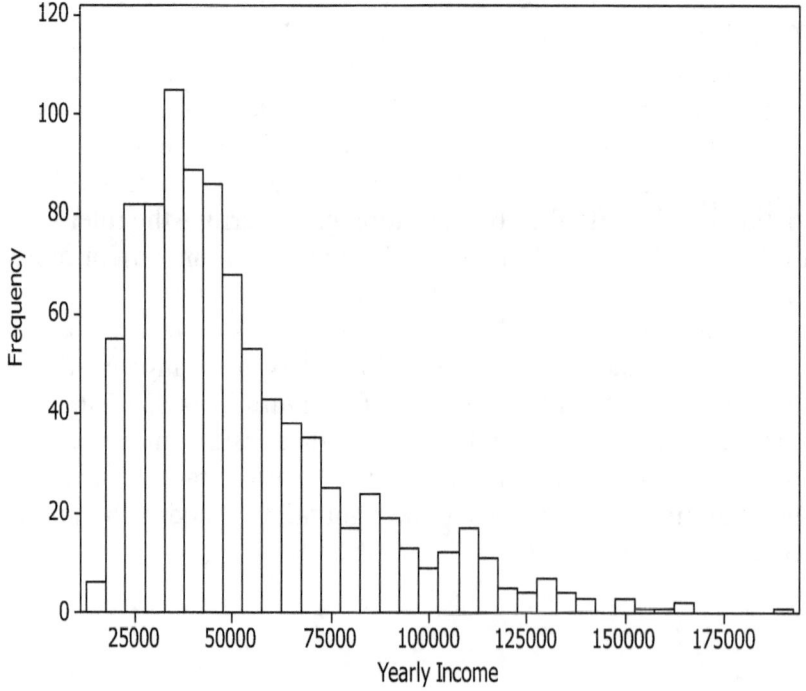

Figure 23. EEACM Wage Structure

deviation of $28,039. Records indicate 354,710 people earn a living in EEACM.

Removing the top 20% of data appears to eliminate these top-heavy influences and returns the data displayed in Figure 24. Average wage structure value has dropped to $41,127 with a corresponding reduction in standard deviation of $13,886. The EEACM Johnson Transformation equation is:

$$0.503715 + 0.952512 * Ln((X - 14273.2) / (64194.6 - X))$$

Evaluating the data range of the lower 80% and the upper 20% shows the upper has more range. There appears inequitable, excessive compensation where the upper 20% of a wage structure has more range than the lower 80% of personnel. In addition, this comparison does not include the more highly paid managers and executives that exceed any of these values. Probability distribution data analysis using the Johnson Transformation results in a P-value of 0.321, confirming a good fit for a normal distribution.

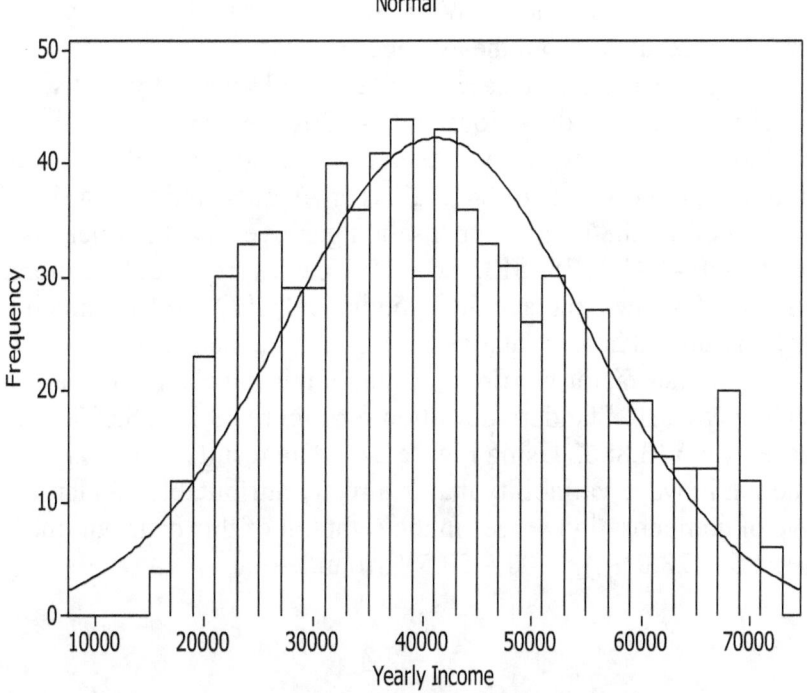

Figure 24. EEACM Normal Curve

Even if one were to consider Figure 23 a fair representation and the top executive (CEO) salary was limited to $1,000,000, it would require over 33 standard deviations to reach the $1,000,000 mark from this larger average: ($1,000,000 - $52,671) / $28,039 = 33.8 standard deviations (rounded).

It is easy to see from observing the charts for EEACM that each one has a different size scale for the x-axis to represent data. The statistical software automatically calculates scale size and provides an output fitting allowable space on a sheet of paper. Comparison of one figure to another in this fashion can be difficult due to scale differences. However, in an attempt to create an example that is easier to conceptualize, reconsider Figure 6. Figure 6 can be used to compare distances of the mean to any value because it places all standard deviations within a uniform distance on its scale. Regardless of standard deviation amount, it takes only one inch of space across the scale. Three standard deviations from the average represent approximately 99.865% of the lower 80% of a workforce. The further we move right, the more rare an individual becomes with a truly unique ability of 1/1,000,000 workers represented at 4.75 (inches) standard deviations. With Figure 23, the CEOs salary is over 2-1/2 feet away from the average.

We considered the case for all data in Figure 23 with its resulting 33 standard deviations and 2-1/2 feet distance to reach $1,000,000, let us now consider the more realistic case of Figure 24. Using the revised values of $41,127 as an average and standard deviation of $13,886, the compensation gap overruns the ruler to ($1,000,000 - $41,127) / $13,886 = 69.1 inches (rounded), or more than 5 feet 9 inches to reach the hypothetical CEO's salary, much more if reality indicates salaries are larger for executives.

Another factor worthy of evaluation is the change in standard deviation values. Standard deviation for Figure 23 is $28,039 and Figure 24 is $13,886. Using Figure 24's data results in a 50% reduction in wage variability that is directly attributable to a large range of compensation values in the right tail of this distribution: (1 - ($13,886 / $28,039)) * 100 = 50.5% (rounded).

Furniture and Related Product Manufacturing

Materials used in these industries include wood, metal, glass, plastics and those processes that cut, bend, mold, and laminate materials into products such as furniture, cabinets, mattresses, vertical and horizontal blinds, and other furniture forms. Fashion and design enter into the creation of end products. Designers, engineers, finishers, managers, carpenters, various machine operators and tenders are common occupations.

Using the data within the Furniture and Related Product industries resulted in a histogram with a long tail to the right as displayed in Figure 25. More bars on the right side that decrease in value than on the left indicate a positively skewed distribution. There are irregular gaps in the right tail.

Remember the dice example where a large number skewed the mean and standard deviation results? We can easily see there are large values in the tail of Figure 25. Using a statistical program to evaluate all data resulted in an average of $43,893 and standard

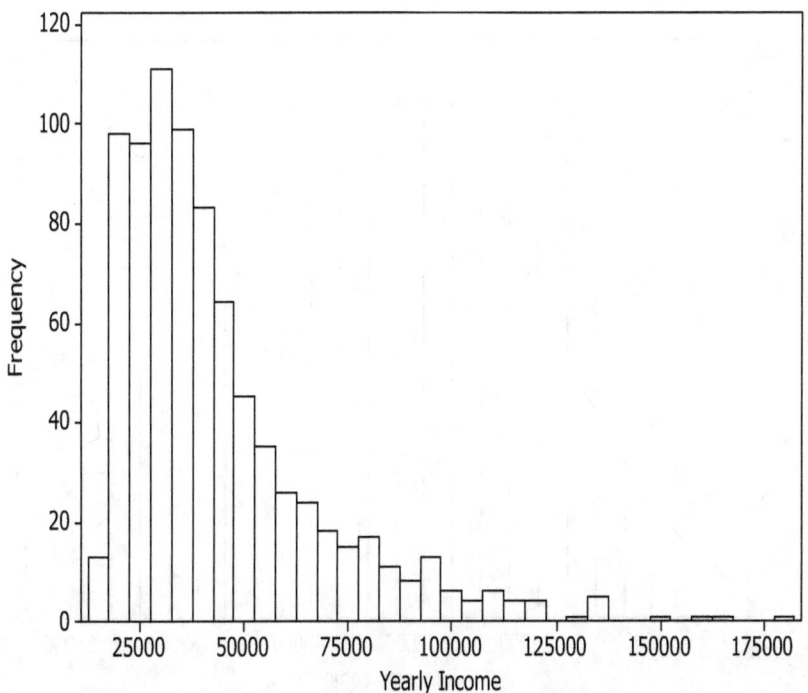

Figure 25. Furniture and Related Products Wage Structure

deviation of $24,394. Records indicate 336,960 people earn a living in Furniture and Related Products.

Removing the top 20% of data appears to eliminate these top-heavy influences and returns the data displayed in Figure 26. Average wage structure value has dropped to $33,888 with a corresponding reduction in standard deviation of $10,635. The Furniture and Related Products Johnson Transformation equation is:

$$0.503715 + 0.952512 * Ln((X - 14273.2) / (64194.6 - X)).$$

Evaluating the data range of the lower 80% and the upper 20% shows the upper has more range. There appears inequitable, excessive compensation where the upper 20% of a wage structure has more range than the lower 80% of personnel. In addition, this comparison does not include the more highly paid managers and executives that exceed any of these values. Probability distribution data analysis using the Johnson Transformation results in a P-value of 0.242, confirming a good fit for a normal distribution.

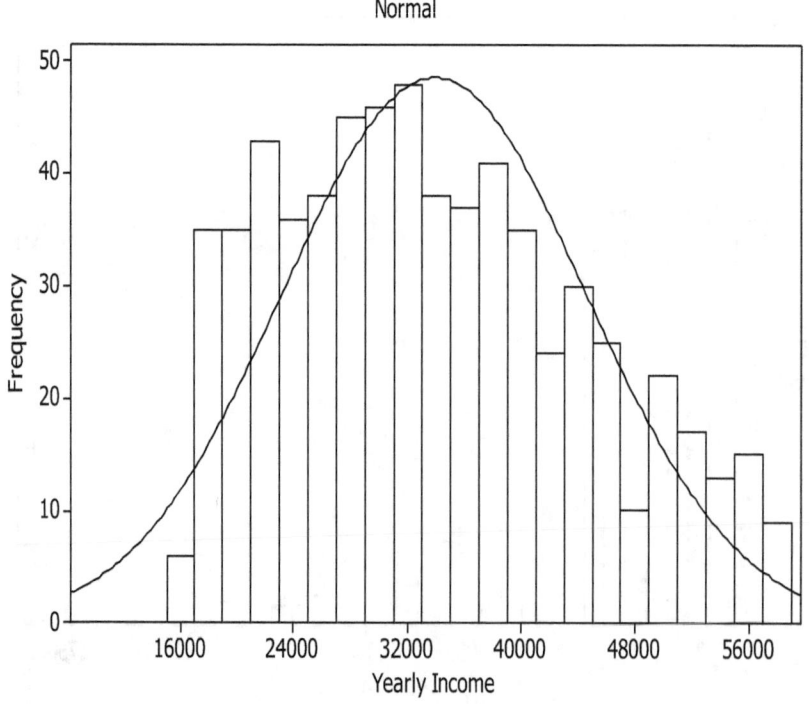

Figure 26. Furniture and Related Products Normal Curve

Even if one were to consider Figure 25 a fair representation and the top executive (CEO) salary was limited to $1,000,000, it would require over 39 standard deviations to reach the $1,000,000 mark from this larger average: ($1,000,000 - $43,893) / $24,394 = 39.2 standard deviations (rounded).

It is easy to see from observing the charts for Furniture and Related Products that each one has a different size scale for the x-axis to represent data. The statistical software automatically calculates scale size and provides an output fitting allowable space on a sheet of paper. Comparison of one figure to another in this fashion can be difficult due to scale differences. However, in an attempt to create an example that is easier to conceptualize, reconsider Figure 6. Figure 6 can be used to compare distances of the mean to any value because it places all standard deviations within a uniform distance on its scale. Regardless of standard deviation amount, it takes only one inch of space across the scale. Three standard deviations from the average represent approximately 99.865% of the lower 80% of a workforce. The further we move right, the more rare an individual becomes with a truly unique ability of 1/1,000,000 workers represented at 4.75 (inches) standard deviations. With Figure 25, the CEOs salary is over 3 <u>feet</u> away from the average.

We considered the case for all data in Figure 25 with its resulting 39 standard deviations and 3 feet 3 inch distance to reach $1,000,000, let us now consider the more realistic case of Figure 26. Using the revised values of $33,888 as an average and standard deviation of $10,635, the compensation gap overruns the ruler to ($1,000,000 - $33,888) / $10,635 = 90.8 inches (rounded), or more than 7 feet 6 inches to reach the hypothetical CEO's salary, much more if reality indicates salaries are larger for executives.

Another factor worthy of evaluation is the change in standard deviation values. Standard deviation for Figure 25 is $24,394 and Figure 26 is $10,635. Using Figure 26's data results in over a 56% reduction in wage variability that is directly attributable to a large range of compensation values in the right tail of this distribution: (1 - ($10,635 / $24,394)) * 100 = 56.4% (rounded).

Furniture and Home Furnishing Stores

Furniture stores and home furnishing stores are the two industry groups under Furniture and Home Furnishing Stores. These are fixed locations where sales occur in a large showroom type of setting. Interior decorator and design functions are frequently incorporated into the services offered customers to create a unique feel and ambiance. Common occupations include supervisors and managers, laborers, salespersons, stock clerks, and truck drivers.

Using the data within the Furniture and Home Furnishing Stores industries resulted in a histogram with a long tail to the right as displayed in Figure 27. More bars on the right side that decrease in value than on the left indicate a positively skewed distribution. There are irregular gaps in the right tail.

Remember the dice example where a large number skewed the mean and standard deviation results? We can easily see there are large values in the tail of Figure 27. Using a statistical program to evaluate all data resulted in an average of $40,705 and standard

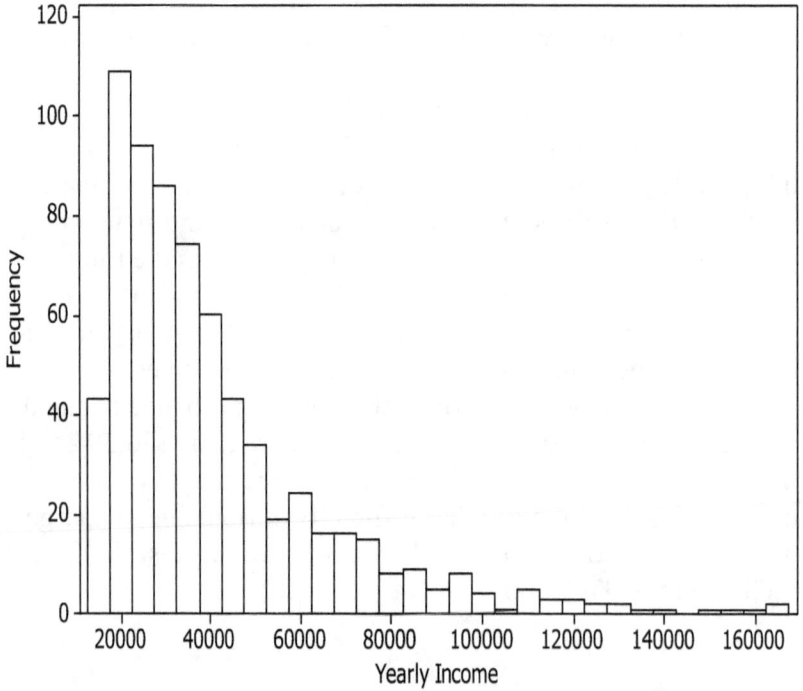

Figure 27. Furniture & Home Furnishing Stores Wage Structure

deviation of $24,914. Records indicate 444,580 people earn a living in Furniture & Home Furnishing Stores.

Removing the top 20% of data appears to eliminate these top-heavy influences and returns the data displayed in Figure 28. Average wage structure value has dropped to $30,556 with a corresponding reduction in standard deviation of $10,260. The Furniture & Home Furnishing Stores Johnson Transformation equation is:

$$0.491426 + 0.722278 * Ln((X - 15241.0) / (55928.4 - X)).$$

Evaluating the data range of the lower 80% and the upper 20% shows the upper has more range. There appears inequitable, excessive compensation where the upper 20% of a wage structure has more range than the lower 80% of personnel. In addition, this comparison does not include the more highly paid managers and executives that exceed any of these values. Probability distribution data analysis using the Johnson Transformation results in a P-value

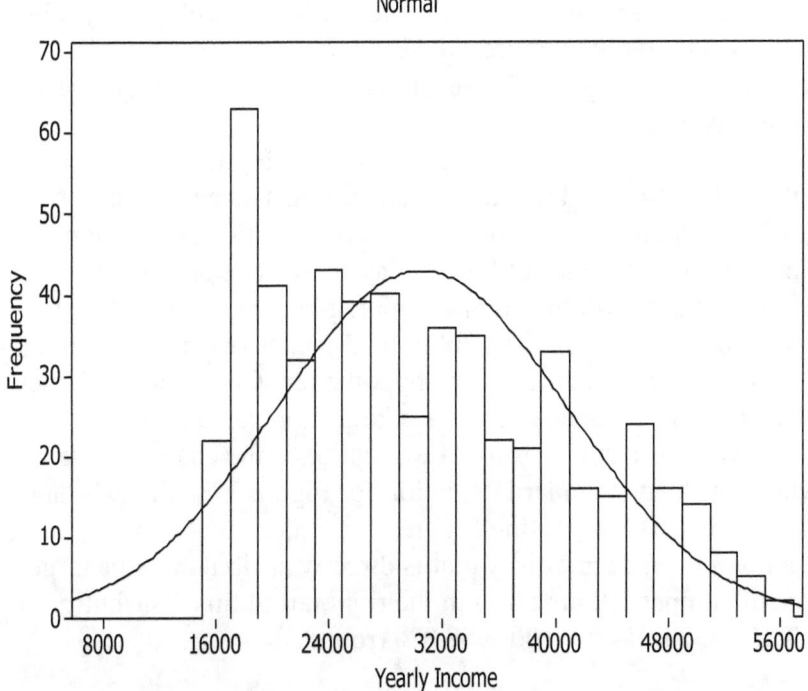

Figure 28. Furniture & Home Furnishing Stores Normal Curve

of 0.418, confirming a good fit for a normal distribution.

Even if one were to consider Figure 27 a fair representation and the top executive (CEO) salary was limited to $1,000,000, it would require over 38 standard deviations to reach the $1,000,000 mark from this larger average: ($1,000,000 - $40,705) / $24,914 = 38.5 standard deviations (rounded).

It is easy to see from observing the charts for Furniture & Home Furnishing Stores that each one has a different size scale for the x-axis to represent data. The statistical software automatically calculates scale size and provides an output fitting allowable space on a sheet of paper. Comparison of one figure to another in this fashion can be difficult due to scale differences. However, in an attempt to create an example that is easier to conceptualize, reconsider Figure 6. Figure 6 can be used to compare distances of the mean to any value because it places all standard deviations within a uniform distance on its scale. Regardless of standard deviation amount, it takes only one inch of space across the scale. Three standard deviations from the average represent approximately 99.865% of the lower 80% of a workforce. The further we move right, the more rare an individual becomes with a truly unique ability of 1/1,000,000 workers represented at 4.75 (inches) standard deviations. With Figure 27, the CEOs salary is over 3 <u>feet</u> away from the average.

We considered the case for all data in Figure 27 with its resulting 38 standard deviations and 3 feet distance to reach $1,000,000, let us now consider the more realistic case of Figure 28. Using the revised values of $30,556 as an average and standard deviation of $10,260, the compensation gap overruns the ruler to ($1,000,000 - $30,556) / $10,260 = 94.5 inches (rounded), or more than 7 feet 10 inches to reach the hypothetical CEO's salary, much more if reality indicates salaries are larger for executives.

Another factor worthy of evaluation is the change in standard deviation values. Standard deviation for Figure 27 is $24,914 and Figure 28 is $10,260. Using Figure 28's data results in over a 58% reduction in wage variability that is directly attributable to a large range of compensation values in the right tail of this distribution: (1 - ($10,260 / $24,914)) * 100 = 58.8% (rounded).

Air Transportation

Industries under Air Transportation are classified into two groups, those that perform their activities on a schedule and those with more flexibility that adhere to nonscheduled transportation operations involving charter, varying operation hours, additional airports served, and a wider range of aircraft used in specialize services. Aircraft mechanics, pilots, flight attendants, cargo agents, and ticket agents are frequent occupations.

Using the data within the Air Transportation industries resulted in a histogram with a long tail to the right as displayed in Figure 29. More bars on the right side that decrease in value than on the left indicate a positively skewed distribution. There are irregular gaps in the right tail.

Remember the dice example where a large number skewed the mean and standard deviation results? We can easily see there are large values in the tail of Figure 29. Using a statistical program to evaluate all data resulted in an average of $55,702 and standard

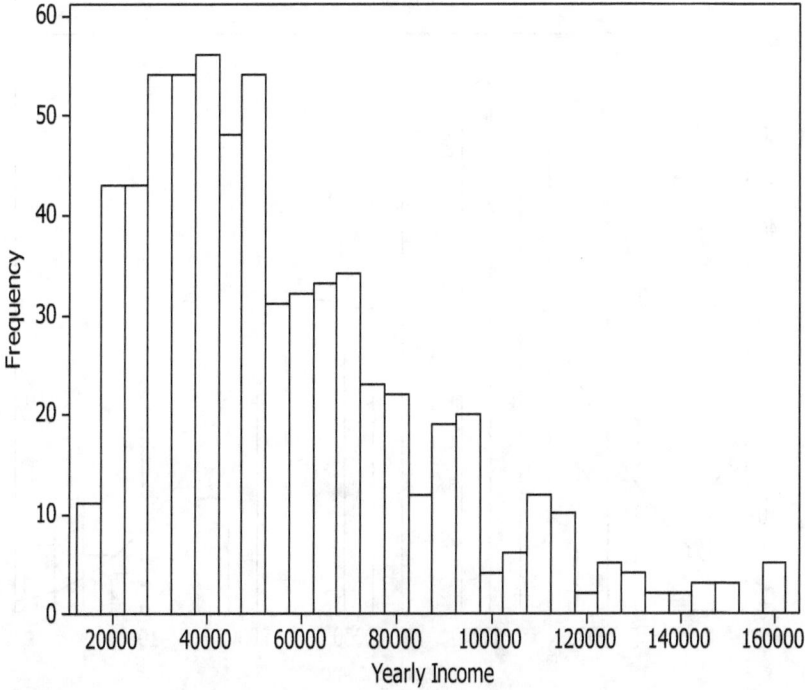

Figure 29. Air Transportation Wage Structure

deviation of $29,611. Records indicate 451,000 people earn a living in Air Transportation.

Removing the top 20% of data appears to eliminate these top-heavy influences and returns the data displayed in Figure 30. Average wage structure value has dropped to $51,899 with a corresponding reduction in standard deviation of $24,172. The Air Transportation Johnson Transformation equation is:

$$0.484233 + 0.847427 * Ln((X - 14768.2) / (69998.0 - X)).$$

Evaluating the data range of the lower 80% and the upper 20% shows the upper has more range. There appears inequitable, excessive compensation where the upper 20% of a wage structure has more range than the lower 80% of personnel. In addition, this comparison does not include the more highly paid managers and executives that exceed any of these values. Probability distribution data analysis using the Johnson Transformation results in a P-value of 0.687, confirming a good fit for a normal distribution.

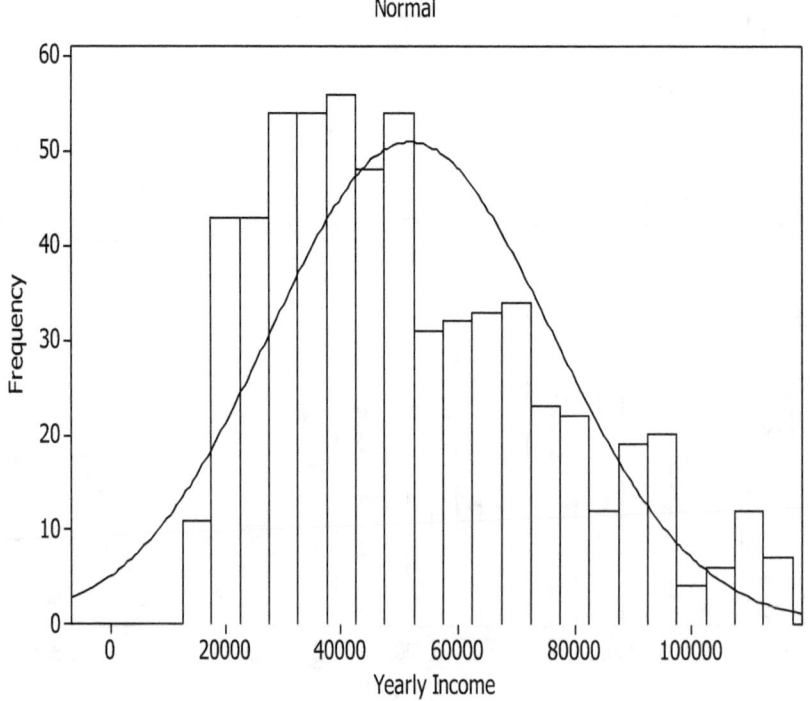

Figure 30. Air Transportation with Normal Curve

Even if one were to consider Figure 29 a fair representation and the top executive (CEO) salary was limited to $1,000,000, it would require over 31 standard deviations to reach the $1,000,000 mark from this larger average: ($1,000,000 - $55,702) / $29,611 = 31.9 standard deviations (rounded).

It is easy to see from observing the charts for Air Transportation that each one has a different size scale for the x-axis to represent data. The statistical software automatically calculates scale size and provides an output fitting allowable space on a sheet of paper. Comparison of one figure to another in this fashion can be difficult due to scale differences. However, in an attempt to create an example that is easier to conceptualize, reconsider Figure 6. Figure 6 can be used to compare distances of the mean to any value because it places all standard deviations within a uniform distance on its scale. Regardless of standard deviation amount, it takes only one inch of space across the scale. Three standard deviations from the average represent approximately 99.865% of the lower 80% of a workforce. The further we move right, the more rare an individual becomes with a truly unique ability of 1/1,000,000 workers represented at 4.75 (inches) standard deviations. With Figure 29, the CEOs salary is over 2-1/2 feet away from the average.

We considered the case for all data in Figure 29 with its resulting 31 standard deviations and 2-1/2 feet distance to reach $1,000,000, let us now consider the more realistic case of Figure 30. Using the revised values of $51,899 as an average and standard deviation of $24,172, the compensation gap overruns the ruler to ($1,000,000 - $51,899) / $24,172 = 39.2 inches (rounded), or more than 3 feet 3 inches to reach the hypothetical CEO's salary, much more if reality indicates salaries are larger for executives. Another factor worthy of evaluation is the change in standard deviation values. Standard deviation for Figure 29 is $29,611 and Figure 30 is $24,172. Using Figure 30's data results in over a 18% reduction in wage variability that is directly attributable to a large range of compensation values in the right tail of this distribution: (1 - ($24,172 / $29,611)) * 100 = 18.4% (rounded).

Warehousing and Storage

Industries within Warehousing and Storage are involved in providing facilities for storage of general merchandise, refrigerated goods, and other products requiring off-site location for varying time periods. Keeping material secure also falls under these industries' responsibility. The term logistics services is frequently applied to these activities and may include large shipment reduction in size and repackaging, inventory control, and coordinating transportation.

Using the data within the Warehousing and Storage industries resulted in a histogram with a long tail to the right as displayed in Figure 31. More bars on the right side that decrease in value than on the left indicate a positively skewed distribution. There are irregular gaps in the right tail.

Remember the dice example where a large number skewed the mean and standard deviation results? We can easily see there are large values in the tail of Figure 31. Using a statistical program to evaluate all data resulted in an average of $47,475 and standard

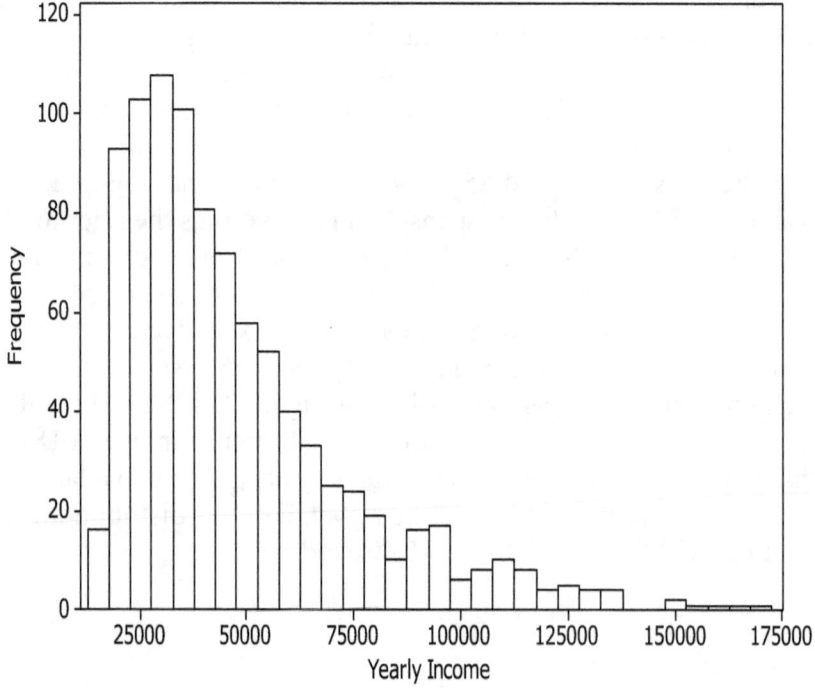

Figure 31. Warehousing and Storage Wage Structure

deviation of $26,455. Records indicate 639,150 people earn a living in Warehousing and Storage.

Removing the top 20% of data appears to eliminate these top-heavy influences and returns the data displayed in Figure 32. Average wage structure value has dropped to $36,629 with a corresponding reduction in standard deviation of $12,676. The Warehousing and Storage Johnson Transformation equation is:

$$0.484233 + 0.847427 * Ln((X - 14768.2) / (69998.0 - X)).$$

Evaluating the data range of the lower 80% and the upper 20% shows the upper has more range. There appears inequitable, excessive compensation where the upper 20% of a wage structure has more range than the lower 80% of personnel. In addition, this comparison does not include the more highly paid managers and executives that exceed any of these values. Probability distribution data analysis using the Johnson Transformation results in a P-value of 0.494, confirming a good fit for a normal distribution.

Even if one were to consider Figure 31 a fair representation and the top executive (CEO) salary was limited to $1,000,000, it would require over 36 standard deviations to reach the $1,000,000 mark from this larger average: ($1,000,000 - $47,475) / $26,455=

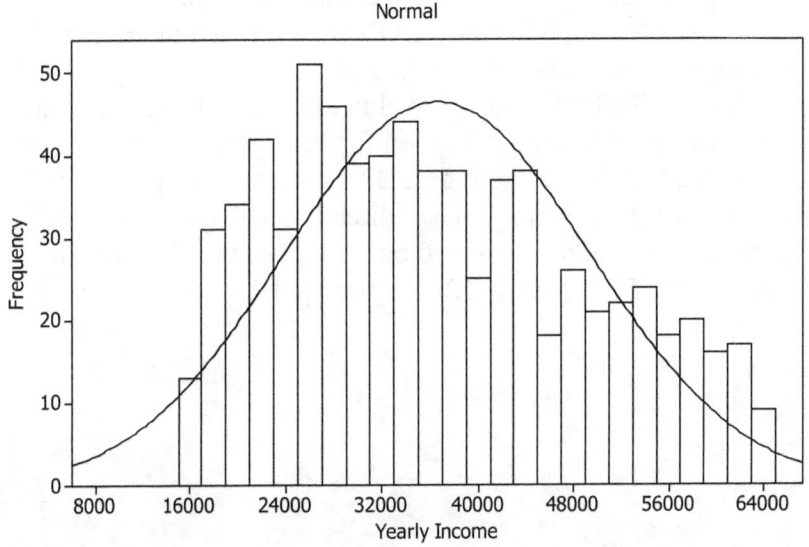

Figure 32. Warehousing and Storage with a Normal Curve

36.0 standard deviations (rounded).

It is easy to see from observing the charts for Warehousing and Storage that each one has a different size scale for the x-axis to represent data. The statistical software automatically calculates scale size and provides an output fitting allowable space on a sheet of paper. Comparison of one figure to another in this fashion can be difficult due to scale differences. However, in an attempt to create an example that is easier to conceptualize, reconsider Figure 6. Figure 6 can be used to compare distances of the mean to any value because it places all standard deviations within a uniform distance on its scale. Regardless of standard deviation amount, it takes only one inch of space across the scale. Three standard deviations from the average represent approximately 99.865% of the lower 80% of a workforce. The further we move right, the more rare an individual becomes with a truly unique ability of 1/1,000,000 workers represented at 4.75 (inches) standard deviations. With Figure 31, the CEOs salary is 3 <u>feet</u> away from the average.

We considered the case for all data in Figure 31 with its resulting 36 standard deviations and 3 feet distance to reach $1,000,000, let us now consider the more realistic case of Figure 32. Using the revised values of $36,629 as an average and standard deviation of $12,676, the compensation gap overruns the ruler to ($1,000,000 - $36,629) / $12,676 = 76.0 inches (rounded), or 6 feet 4 inches to reach the hypothetical CEO's salary, much more if reality indicates salaries are larger for executives.

Another factor worthy of evaluation is the change in standard deviation values. Standard deviation for Figure 31 is $26,455 and Figure 32 is $12,676. Using Figure 32's data results in over a 52% reduction in wage variability that is directly attributable to a large range of compensation values in the right tail of this distribution: (1 - ($12,676 / $26,455)) * 100 = 52.1% (rounded).

Publishing Industries

Industries in this group are not involve in activities related to internet publishing. Activities include publishing various periodicals, books, mailing list, and software. Technology allows using traditional printing, CD-ROMs, or other electronic methods to convey information. Published materials may include works created by authors outside the company or in-house. Editors, graphic designers, and software engineers are frequent occupations.

Using the data within the Publishing Industries resulted in a histogram with a long tail to the right as displayed in Figure 33. More bars on the right side that decrease in value than on the left indicate a positively skewed distribution. There are irregular gaps in the right tail.

Remember the dice example where a large number skewed the mean and standard deviation results? We can easily see there are large values in the tail of Figure 33. Using a statistical program to evaluate all data resulted in an average of $56,125 and standard

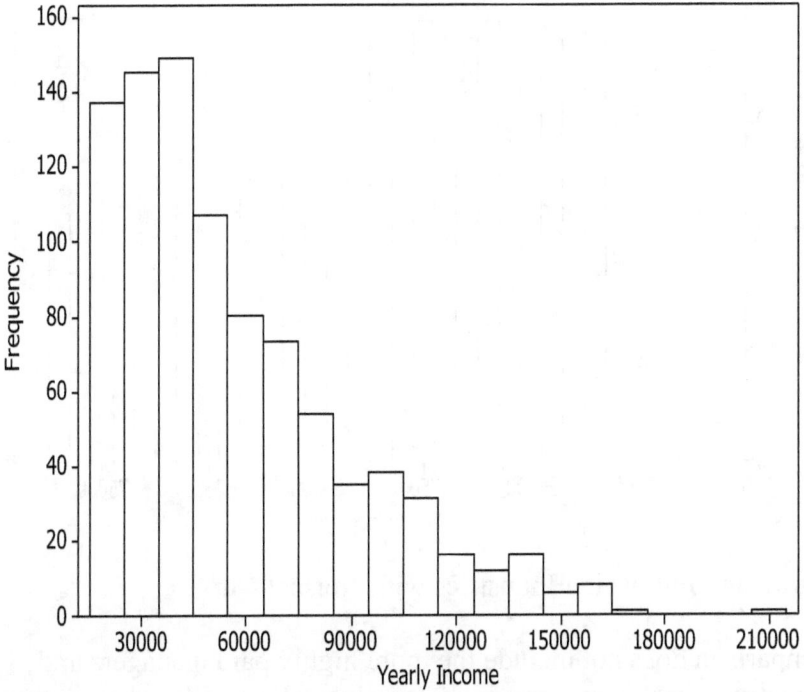

Figure 33. Publishing Industries Wage Structure

deviation of $32,953. Records indicate 758,090 people earn a living in Publishing Industries.

      Removing the top 20% of data appears to eliminate these top-heavy influences and returns the data displayed in Figure 34. Average wage structure value has dropped to $42,585 with a corresponding reduction in standard deviation of $17,650. The Publishing Industries Johnson Transformation equation is:

$$0.513649 + 0.827868 * Ln((X - 13973.9) / (65883.4 - X)).$$

      Evaluating the data range of the lower 80% and the upper 20% shows the upper has more range. There appears inequitable, excessive compensation where the upper 20% of a wage structure has more range than the lower 80% of personnel. In addition, this

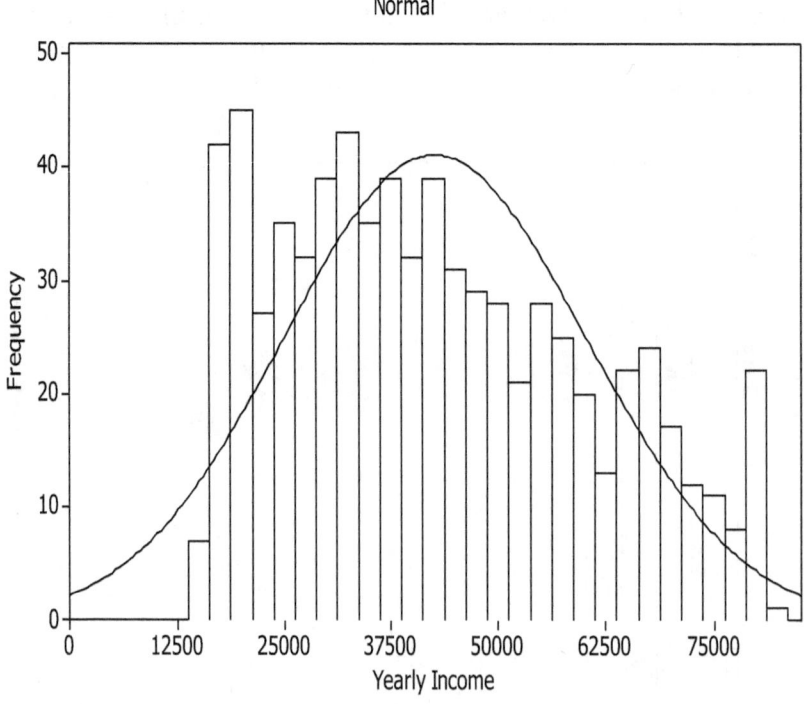

Figure 34. Publishing Industries with Normal Curve

comparison does not include the more highly paid managers and executives that exceed any of these values. Probability distribution data analysis using the Johnson Transformation results in a P-value

of 0.125, confirming a good fit for a normal distribution.

Even if one were to consider Figure 33 a fair representation and the top executive (CEO) salary was limited to $1,000,000, it would require over 28 standard deviations to reach the $1,000,000 mark from this larger average: ($1,000,000 - $56,125) / $32,953 = 28.6 standard deviations (rounded).

It is easy to see from observing the charts for Publishing Industries that each one has a different size scale for the x-axis to represent data. The statistical software automatically calculates scale size and provides an output fitting allowable space on a sheet of paper. Comparison of one figure to another in this fashion can be difficult due to scale differences. However, in an attempt to create an example that is easier to conceptualize, reconsider Figure 6. Figure 6 can be used to compare distances of the mean to any value because it places all standard deviations within a uniform distance on its scale. Regardless of standard deviation amount, it takes only one inch of space across the scale. Three standard deviations from the average represent approximately 99.865% of the lower 80% of a workforce. The further we move right, the more rare an individual becomes with a truly unique ability of 1/1,000,000 workers represented at 4.75 (inches) standard deviations. With Figure33, the CEOs salary is over 2 <u>feet</u> away from the average.

We considered the case for all data in Figure 33 with its resulting 28 standard deviations and 2 feet distance to reach $1,000,000, let us now consider the more realistic case of Figure 34. Using the revised values of $42,585 as an average and standard deviation of $17,650, the compensation gap overruns the ruler to ($1,000,000 - $42,585) / $17,650 = 54.2 inches (rounded), or more than 4 feet 6 inches to reach the hypothetical CEO's salary, much more if reality indicates salaries are larger for executives.

Another factor worthy of evaluation is the change in standard deviation values. Standard deviation for Figure 33 is $32,953 and Figure 34 is $17,650. Using Figure 34's data results in a 46% reduction in wage variability that is directly attributable to a large range of compensation values in the right tail of this distribution: (1 - ($17,650 / $32,953)) * 100 = 46.4% (rounded).

Telecommunications

These industries work to provide services related to telephone, cable and satellite program services, and internet services. Activities focus on providing access to facilities for the purpose of conveying voice, data, text, sound, video, as well as operating these facilities. Customer service representatives, electronic engineers, supervisors and managers, equipment installers, maintenance, and administrative support are common occupations.

Using the data within the Telecommunications industries resulted in a histogram with a long tail to the right as displayed in Figure 35. More bars on the right side that decrease in value than on the left indicate a positively skewed distribution. There are irregular gaps in the right tail.

Remember the dice example where a large number skewed the mean and standard deviation results? We can easily see there are large values in the tail of Figure 35. Using a statistical program to evaluate all data resulted in an average of $60,223 and standard

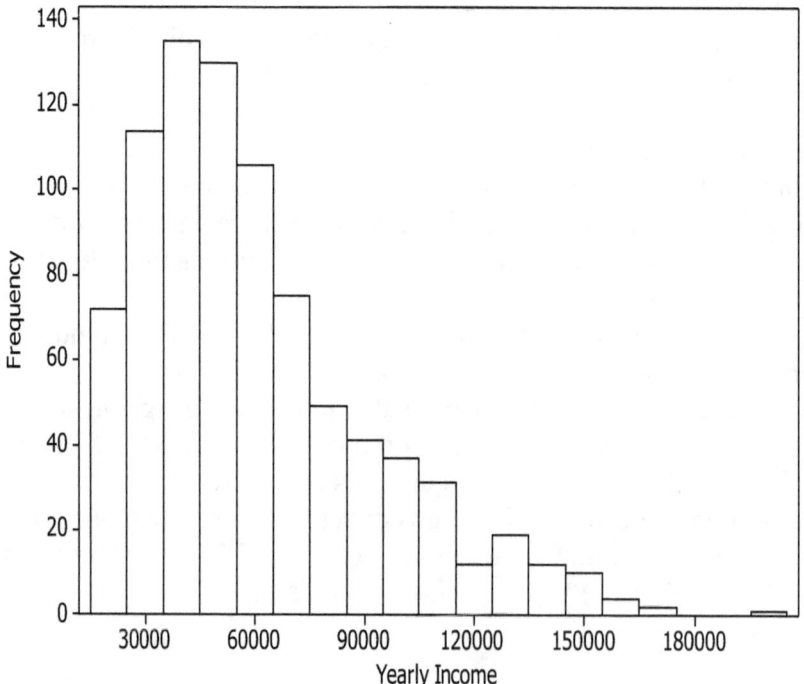

Figure 35. Telecommunications Wage Structure

deviation of $31,745. Records indicate 909,780 people earn a living in Telecommunications.

Removing the top 20% of data appears to eliminate these top-heavy influences and returns the data displayed in Figure 36. Average wage structure value has dropped to $47,226 with a corresponding reduction in standard deviation of $17,235. The Telecommunications Johnson Transformation equation is:

$$0.513649 + 0.827868 * Ln((X - 13973.9) / (65883.4 - X)).$$

Evaluating the data range of the lower 80% and the upper 20% shows the upper has more range. There appears inequitable, excessive compensation where the upper 20% of a wage structure has more range than the lower 80% of personnel. In addition, this comparison does not include the more highly paid managers and executives that exceed any of these values. Probability distribution data analysis using the Johnson Transformation results in a P-value of 0.353, confirming a good fit for a normal distribution.

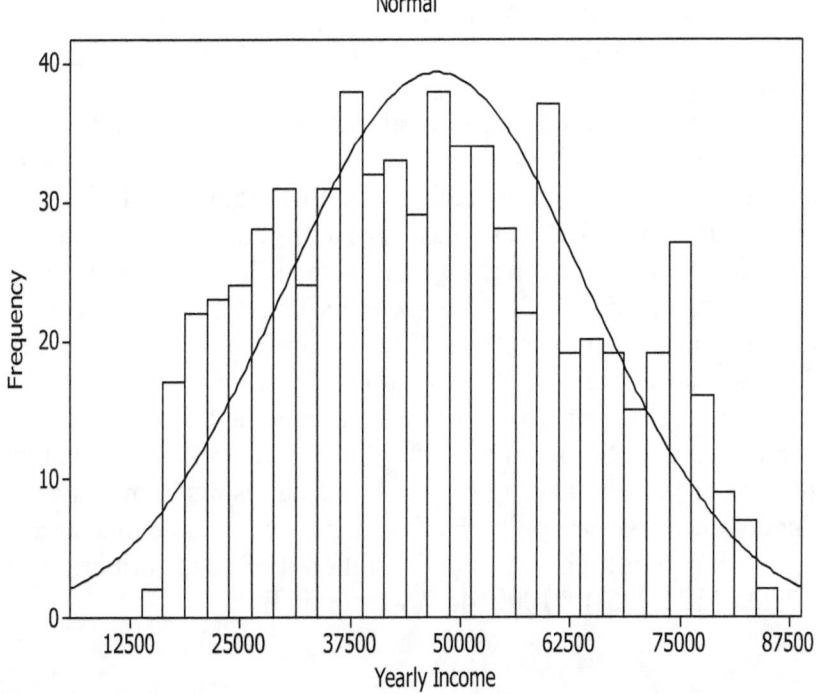

Figure 36. Telecommunications Normal Curve

Even if one were to consider Figure 35 a fair representation and the top executive (CEO) salary was limited to $1,000,000, it would require over 29 standard deviations to reach the $1,000,000 mark from this larger average: ($1,000,000 - $60,223) / $31,745 = 29.6 standard deviations (rounded).

It is easy to see from observing the charts for Telecommunications that each one has a different size scale for the x-axis to represent data. The statistical software automatically calculates scale size and provides an output fitting allowable space on a sheet of paper. Comparison of one figure to another in this fashion can be difficult due to scale differences. However, in an attempt to create an example that is easier to conceptualize, reconsider Figure 6. Figure 6 can be used to compare distances of the mean to any value because it places all standard deviations within a uniform distance on its scale. Regardless of standard deviation amount, it takes only one inch of space across the scale. Three standard deviations from the average represent approximately 99.865% of the lower 80% of a workforce. The further we move right, the more rare an individual becomes with a truly unique ability of 1/1,000,000 workers represented at 4.75 (inches) standard deviations. With Figure 35, the CEOs salary is well over 2 _feet_ away from the average.

We considered the case for all data in Figure 35 with its resulting 29 standard deviations 2 feet distance to reach $1,000,000, let us now consider the more realistic case of Figure 36. Using the revised values of $47,226 as an average and standard deviation of $17,235, the compensation gap overruns the ruler to ($1,000,000 - $47,226) / $17,235 = 55.3 inches (rounded), or more than 4 feet 7 inches to reach the hypothetical CEO's salary, much more if reality indicates salaries are larger for executives.

Another factor worthy of evaluation is the change in standard deviation values. Standard deviation for Figure 35 is $31,745 and Figure 36 is $17,235. Using Figure 36's data results in over a 45% reduction in wage variability that is directly attributable to a large range of compensation values in the right tail of this distribution: (1 - ($17,235 / $31,745)) * 100 = 45.7% (rounded).

Data Processing, Hosting, and Related Services

Industries within data processing, hosting and related services focus attention to establishing and providing the infrastructure needed for hosting or providing data processing services and some may perform both functions. Common occupations include computer programmers, IT system analysts, software development engineers for specific applications or systems.

Using the data within the Data Processing, Hosting, and Related Services (DPH&RS) industries resulted in a histogram with a long tail to the right as displayed in Figure 37. More bars on the right side that decrease in value than on the left indicate a positively skewed distribution. There are irregular gaps in the right tail.

Remember the dice example where a large number skewed the mean and standard deviation results? We can easily see there are large values in the tail of Figure 37. Using a statistical program to evaluate all data resulted in an average of $58,188 and standard deviation of $33,650. Records indicate 239,850 people earn a living

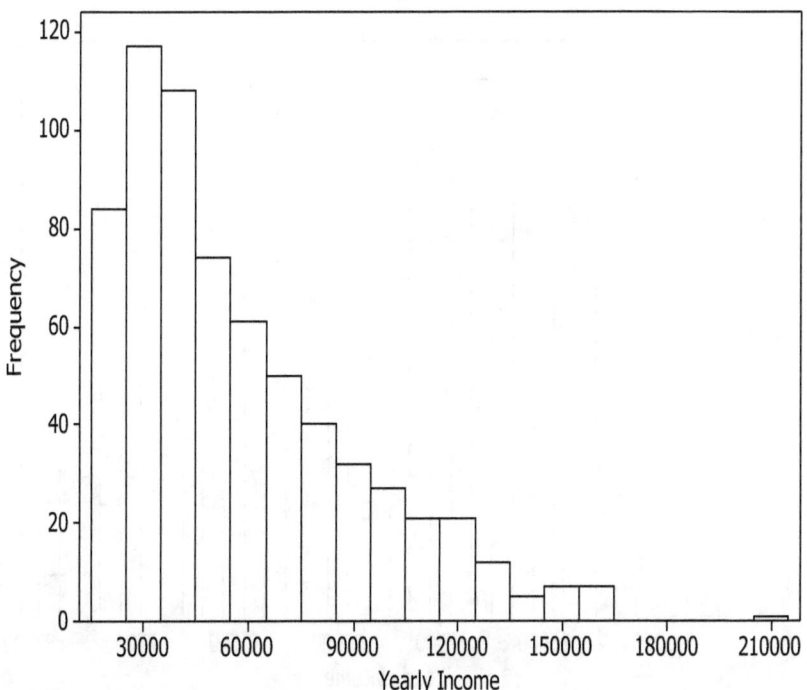

Figure 37. DPH&RS Wage Structure

in DPH&RS.

Removing the top 20% of data appears to eliminate these top-heavy influences and returns the data displayed in Figure 38. Average wage structure value has dropped to $44,325 with a corresponding reduction in standard deviation of $18,222. The DPH&RS Johnson Transformation equation is:

$$0.513649 + 0.827868 * Ln((X - 13973.9) / (65883.4 - X)).$$

Evaluating the data range of the lower 80% and the upper 20% shows the upper has more range. There appears inequitable, excessive compensation where the upper 20% of a wage structure has more range than the lower 80% of personnel. In addition, this comparison does not include the more highly paid managers and executives that exceed any of these values. Probability distribution data analysis using the Johnson Transformation results in a P-value of 0.280, confirming a good fit for a normal distribution.

Even if one were to consider Figure 37 a fair representation

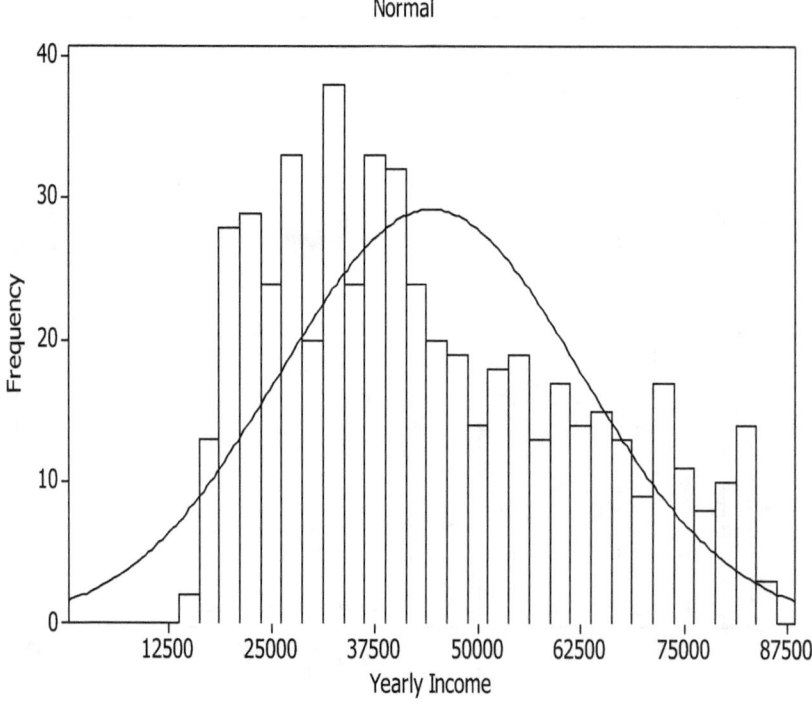

Figure 38. DPH&RS Normal Curve

and the top executive (CEO) salary was limited to $1,000,000, it would require 28 standard deviations to reach the $1,000,000 mark from this larger average: ($1,000,000 - $58,188) / $33,650 = 28.0 standard deviations (rounded).

It is easy to see from observing the charts for DPH&RS that each one has a different size scale for the x-axis to represent data. The statistical software automatically calculates scale size and provides an output fitting allowable space on a sheet of paper. Comparison of one figure to another in this fashion can be difficult due to scale differences. However, in an attempt to create an example that is easier to conceptualize, reconsider Figure 6. Figure 6 can be used to compare distances of the mean to any value because it places all standard deviations within a uniform distance on its scale. Regardless of standard deviation amount, it takes only one inch of space across the scale. Three standard deviations from the average represent approximately 99.865% of the lower 80% of a workforce. The further we move right, the more rare an individual becomes with a truly unique ability of 1/1,000,000 workers represented at 4.75 (inches) standard deviations. With Figure 37, the CEOs salary is over 2 <u>feet</u> away from the average.

We considered the case for all data in Figure 37 with its resulting 28 standard deviations and over 2 feet distance to reach $1,000,000, let us now consider the more realistic case of Figure 38. Using the revised values of $44,325 as an average and standard deviation of $18,222, the compensation gap overruns the ruler to ($1,000,000 - $44,325) / $18,222 = 52.4 inches (rounded), or more than 4 feet 4 inches to reach the hypothetical CEO's salary, much more if reality indicates salaries are larger for executives.

Another factor worthy of evaluation is the change in standard deviation values. Standard deviation for Figure 37 is $33,650 and Figure 38 is $18,222. Using Figure 38's data results in over a 45% reduction in wage variability that is directly attributable to a large range of compensation values in the right tail of this distribution: (1 - ($18,222 / $33,650)) * 100 = 45.8% (rounded).

Rental and Leasing Services

Tangible good for the purpose of leasing or renting is a focal point of industries within rental and leasing services. These goods may include computers, automobiles, industrial machinery, and specialized construction equipment. These industries are segregated into two functions, those that lease, and those that rent. Clerks, supervisors and managers, sales personnel, delivery operations, truck drivers, and vehicle cleaners are some occupations in this area.

Using the data within the Rental and Leasing Services industries resulted in a histogram with a long tail to the right as displayed in Figure 39. More bars on the right side that decrease in value than on the left indicate a positively skewed distribution. There are irregular gaps in the right tail.

Remember the dice example where a large number skewed the mean and standard deviation results? We can easily see there are large values in the tail of Figure 39. Using a statistical program to evaluate all data resulted in an average of $44,835 and standard

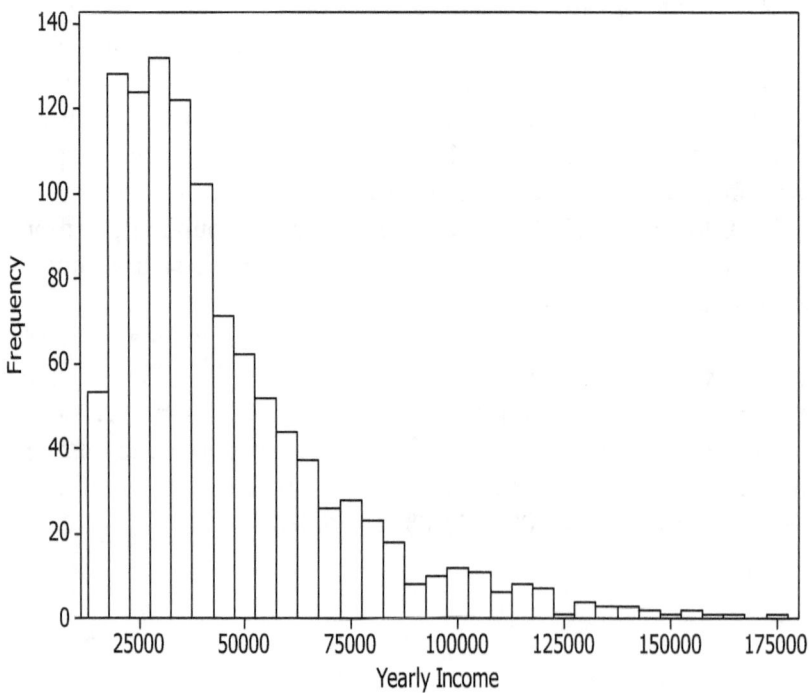

Figure 39. Rental and Leasing Services Wage Structure

deviation of $26,197. Records indicate 517,440 people earn a living in Rental and Leasing Services.

Removing the top 20% of data appears to eliminate these top-heavy influences and returns the data displayed in Figure 40. Average wage structure value has dropped to $34,130 with a corresponding reduction in standard deviation of $12,093. The Rental and Leasing Services Johnson Transformation equation is:

$$0.513649 + 0.827868 * Ln((X - 13973.9) / (65883.4 - X)).$$

Evaluating the data range of the lower 80% and the upper 20% shows the upper has more range. There appears inequitable, excessive compensation where the upper 20% of a wage structure has more range than the lower 80% of personnel. In addition, this

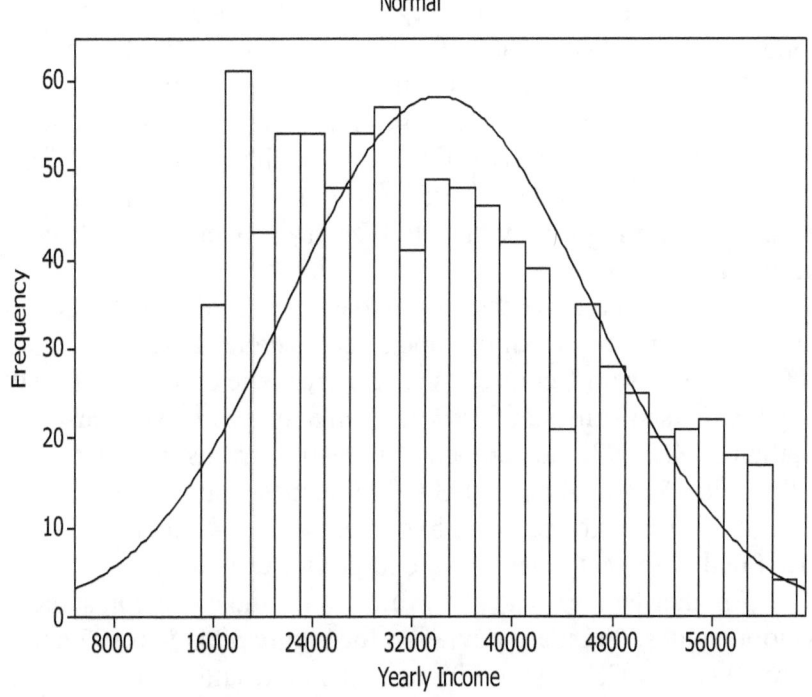

Figure 40. Rental and Leasing Services Normal Curve

comparison does not include the more highly paid managers and executives that exceed any of these values. Probability distribution data analysis using the Johnson Transformation results in a P-value

of 0.172, confirming a good fit for a normal distribution.

Even if one were to consider Figure 39 a fair representation and the top executive (CEO) salary was limited to $1,000,000, it would require over 36 standard deviations to reach the $1,000,000 mark from this larger average: ($1,000,000 - $44,835) / $26,197 = 36.5 standard deviations (rounded).

It is easy to see from observing the charts for Rental and Leasing Services that each one has a different size scale for the x-axis to represent data. The statistical software automatically calculates scale size and provides an output fitting allowable space on a sheet of paper. Comparison of one figure to another in this fashion can be difficult due to scale differences. However, in an attempt to create an example that is easier to conceptualize, reconsider Figure 6. Figure 6 can be used to compare distances of the mean to any value because it places all standard deviations within a uniform distance on its scale. Regardless of standard deviation amount, it takes only one inch of space across the scale. Three standard deviations from the average represent approximately 99.865% of the lower 80% of a workforce. The further we move right, the more rare an individual becomes with a truly unique ability of 1/1,000,000 workers represented at 4.75 (inches) standard deviations. With Figure 39, the CEOs salary is over 3 <u>feet</u> away from the average.

We considered the case for all data in Figure 39 with its resulting 36 standard deviations and 3 feet distance to reach $1,000,000, let us now consider the more realistic case of Figure 40. Using the revised values of $34,130 as an average and standard deviation of $12,093, the compensation gap overruns the ruler to ($1,000,000 - $34,130) / $12,093 = 79.9 inches (rounded), or more than 6 feet 7 inches to reach the hypothetical CEO's salary, much more if reality indicates salaries are larger for executives.

Another factor worthy of evaluation is the change in standard deviation values. Standard deviation for Figure 39 is $26,197 and Figure 40 is $12,093. Using Figure 40's data results in over a 53% reduction in wage variability that is directly attributable to a large range of compensation values in the right tail of this distribution: (1 - ($12,093 / $26,197)) * 100 = 53.8% (rounded).

6 INDUSTRIES OVER 1,000,000 EMPLOYEES

This chapter expands the number of industries evaluated in the United States to include those with more than 1,000,000 employees. Thirteen industries described in this chapter represent almost 33 million employees with many corporations operating in these areas. These industries are a very diverse grouping with people possessing a broad range of interests, experience, educational backgrounds, training, and industry knowledge. There is an occupational list in the appendix covering general functional titles.

Though these industries represent over one-million workers, none of the companies has this level of employment. Addressing the significance of this fact takes place later in this text when setting metrics. A normal distribution chart is in the appendix for referencing the data discussion of each industry.

Building Construction

True to its name, building construction focuses on constructing new buildings, but may involve renovations, alterations, and maintenance and repair functions. Some functions may include on-site assembly of prefabricated buildings, temporary building construction, and panelized units. All or a large percentage of this work may be subcontracted to outside construction companies in the specialty trades.

Using the data within the Building Construction industries resulted in a histogram with a long tail to the right as displayed in Figure 41. More bars on the right side that decrease in value than on the left indicate a positively skewed distribution. There are irregular gaps in the right tail.

Remember the dice example where a large number skewed the mean and standard deviation results? We can easily see there are large values in the tail of Figure 41. Using a statistical program to evaluate all data resulted in an average of $51,844 and standard

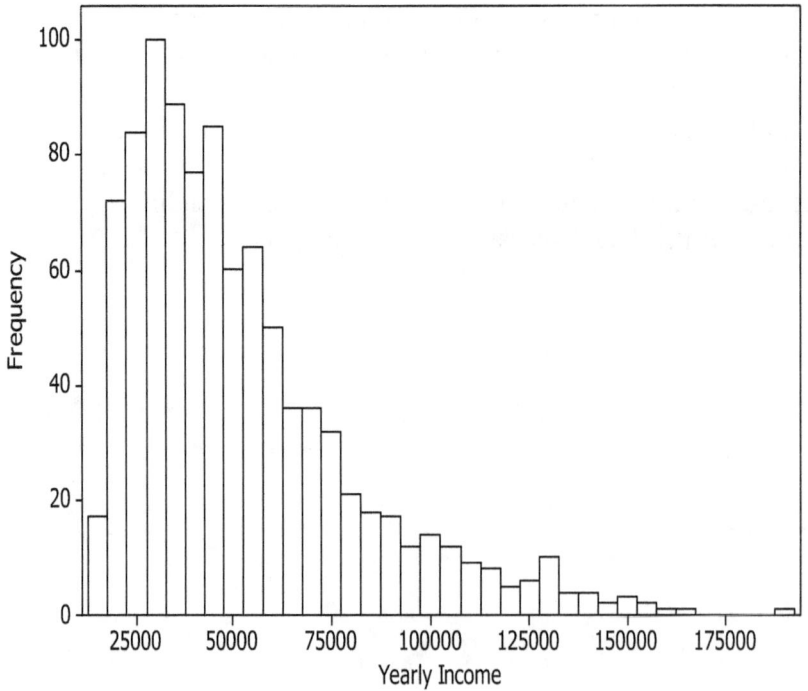

Figure 41. Building Construction Wage Structure

deviation of $28,617. Records indicate 1,255,000 people earn a living in Building Construction.

Removing the top 20% of data appears to eliminate these top-heavy influences and returns the data displayed in Figure 42. Average wage structure value has dropped to $40,207 with a corresponding reduction in standard deviation of $14,450. The Building Construction Johnson Transformation equation is:

$$0.325726 + 0.837870 * Ln((X - 14143.0) / (75953.6 - X)).$$

Evaluating the data range of the lower 80% and the upper 20% shows the upper has more range. There appears inequitable, excessive compensation where the upper 20% of a wage structure has more range than the lower 80% of personnel. In addition, this comparison does not include the more highly paid managers and executives that exceed any of these values. Probability distribution data analysis using the Johnson Transformation results in a P-value of 0.683, confirming a good fit for a normal distribution.

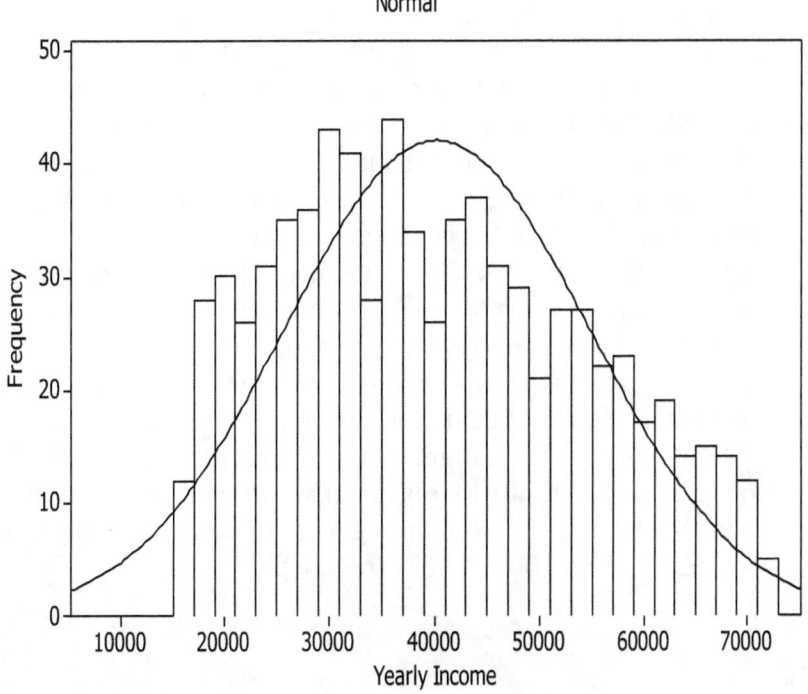

Figure 42. Building Construction Normal Curve

Even if one were to consider Figure 41 a fair representation and the top executive (CEO) salary was limited to $1,000,000, it would require over 33 standard deviations to reach the $1,000,000 mark from this larger average: ($1,000,000 - $51,844) / $28,617 = 33.1 standard deviations (rounded).

It is easy to see from observing the charts for Building Construction that each one has a different size scale for the x-axis to represent data. The statistical software automatically calculates scale size and provides an output fitting allowable space on a sheet of paper. Comparison of one figure to another in this fashion can be difficult due to scale differences. However, in an attempt to create an example that is easier to conceptualize, reconsider Figure 6. Figure 6 can be used to compare distances of the mean to any value because it places all standard deviations within a uniform distance on its scale. Regardless of standard deviation amount, it takes only one inch of space across the scale. Three standard deviations from the average represent approximately 99.865% of the lower 80% of a workforce. The further we move right, the more rare an individual becomes with a truly unique ability of 1/1,000,000 workers represented at 4.75 (inches) standard deviations. With Figure 41, the CEOs salary is over 2-1/2 feet away from the average.

We considered the case for all data in Figure 41 with its resulting 33 standard deviations and 2-1/2 feet distance to reach $1,000,000, let us now consider the more realistic case of Figure 42. Using the revised values of $40,207 as an average and standard deviation of $14,450, the compensation gap overruns the ruler to ($1,000,000 - $40,207) / $14,450 = 66.4 inches (rounded), or more than 5 feet 6 inches to reach the hypothetical CEO's salary, much more if reality indicates salaries are larger for executives.

Another factor worthy of evaluation is the change in standard deviation values. Standard deviation for Figure 41 is $28,617 and Figure 42 is $14,450. Using Figure 42's data results in over a 49% reduction in wage variability that is directly attributable to a large range of compensation values in the right tail of this distribution: (1 - ($14,450 / $28,617)) * 100 = 49.5% (rounded).

Specialty Trade Contractors

Industries in this group usually perform specific tasks that are related to all construction types and are subcontracted specialties such as placement of concrete, plumbing, electrical contracting and so on that do not include completion of an entire project. These activities may include new work, alterations to existing structures, additions, and maintenance and repair functions. Work performed can be for major contractors or property owners.

Using the data within the Specialty Trade Contractors industries resulted in a histogram with a long tail to the right as displayed in Figure 43. More bars on the right side that decrease in value than on the left indicate a positively skewed distribution. There are irregular gaps in the right tail.

Remember the dice example where a large number skewed the mean and standard deviation results? We can easily see there are large values in the tail of Figure 43. Using a statistical program to evaluate all data resulted in an average of $46,339 and standard

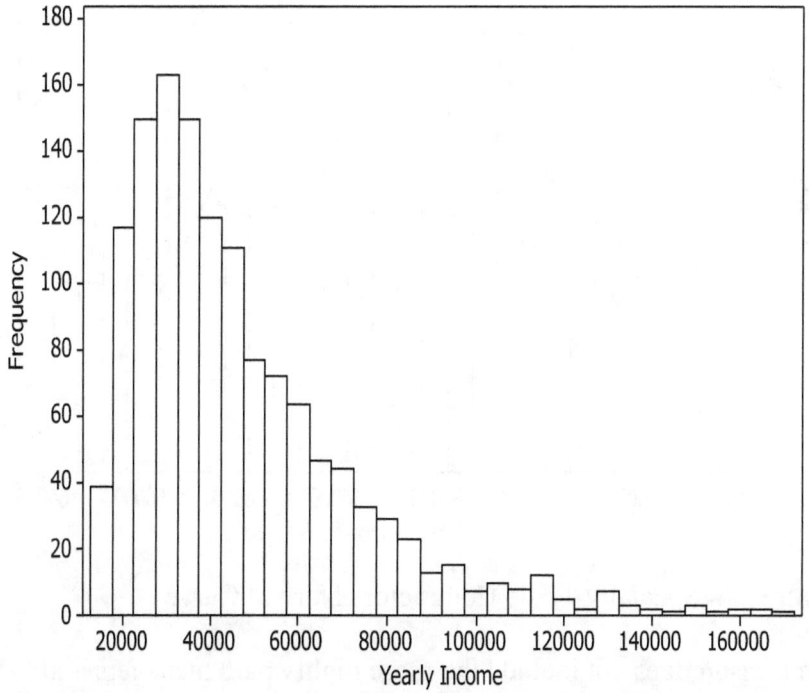

Figure 43. Specialty Trade Contractors Wage Structure

deviation of $25,424. Records indicate 3,566,700 people earn a living in Specialty Trade Contractors.

Removing the top 20% of data appears to eliminate these top-heavy influences and returns the data displayed in Figure 44. Average wage structure value has dropped to $36,107 with a corresponding reduction in standard deviation of $12,295. The Specialty Trade Contractors Johnson Transformation equation is:

$$0.417980 + 0.841066 * Ln((X - 14404.7) / (67679.5 - X)).$$

Evaluating the data range of the lower 80% and the upper 20% shows the upper has more range. There appears inequitable, excessive compensation where the upper 20% of a wage structure has more range than the lower 80% of personnel. In addition, this

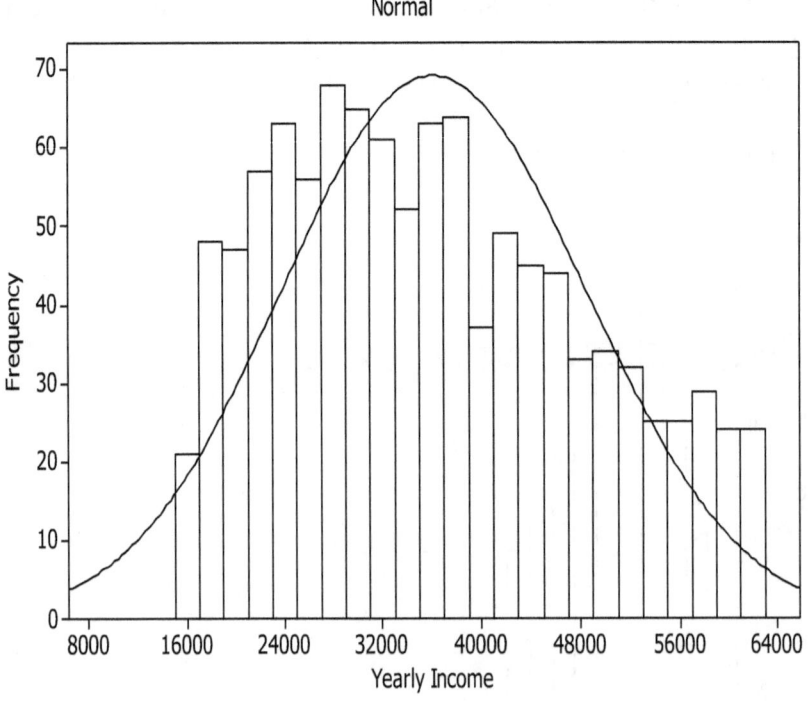

Figure 44. Specialty Trade Contractors Normal Curve

comparison does not include the more highly paid managers and executives that exceed any of these values. Probability distribution data analysis using the Johnson Transformation results in a P-value

of 0.204, confirming a good fit for a normal distribution.

Even if one were to consider Figure 43 a fair representation and the top executive (CEO) salary was limited to $1,000,000, it would require over 37 standard deviations to reach the $1,000,000 mark from this larger average: ($1,000,000 - $46,339) / $25,424 = 37.5 standard deviations (rounded).

It is easy to see from observing the charts for Specialty Trade Contractors that each one has a different size scale for the x-axis to represent data. The statistical software automatically calculates scale size and provides an output fitting allowable space on a sheet of paper. Comparison of one figure to another in this fashion can be difficult due to scale differences. However, in an attempt to create an example that is easier to conceptualize, reconsider Figure 6. Figure 6 can be used to compare distances of the mean to any value because it places all standard deviations within a uniform distance on its scale. Regardless of standard deviation amount, it takes only one inch of space across the scale. Three standard deviations from the average represent approximately 99.865% of the lower 80% of a workforce. The further we move right, the more rare an individual becomes with a truly unique ability of 1/1,000,000 workers represented at 4.75 (inches) standard deviations. With Figure 43, the CEOs salary is over 3 <u>feet</u> away from the average.

We considered the case for all data in Figure 43 with its resulting 37 standard deviations and 3 feet distance to reach $1,000,000, let us now consider the more realistic case of Figure 44. Using the revised values of $36,107 as an average and standard deviation of $12,295, the compensation gap overruns the ruler to ($1,000,000 - $36,107) / $12,295 = 78.4 inches (rounded), or more than 6 feet 6 inches to reach the hypothetical CEO's salary, much more if reality indicates salaries are larger for executives.

Another factor worthy of evaluation is the change in standard deviation values. Standard deviation for Figure 43 is $25,424 and Figure 44 is $12,295. Using Figure 44's data results in over a 51% reduction in wage variability that is directly attributable to a large range of compensation values in the right tail of this distribution: (1 - ($12,295 / $25,424) * 100 = 51.6% (rounded).

Food Manufacturing

Industries in Food Manufacturing focus on changing livestock and agriculture materials into products for consumption at the intermediate and final stages of production. These products are delivered to wholesalers or retailers for sale to customers. Bakeries and candy confectioners not selling directly for consumption are part of these industries. Occupations within this area are bakers, food batch makers, slaughterers and meat packers among others.

Using the data within the Food Manufacturing industries resulted in a histogram with a long tail to the right as displayed in Figure 45. More bars on the right side that decrease in value than on the left indicate a positively skewed distribution. There are irregular gaps in the right tail.

Remember the dice example where a large number skewed the mean and standard deviation results? We can easily see there are large values in the tail of Figure 45. Using a statistical program to evaluate all data resulted in an average of $45,143 and standard

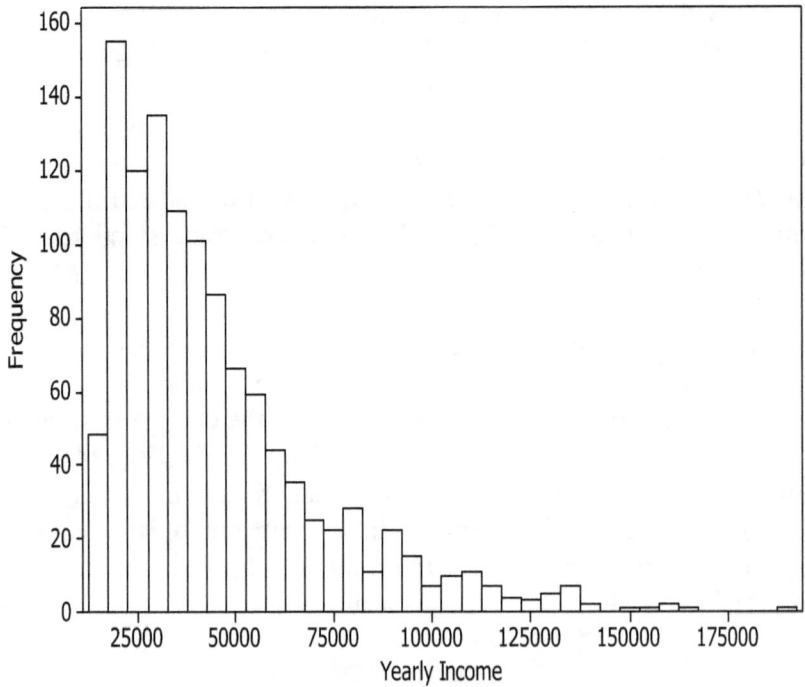

Figure 45. Food Manufacturing Wage Structure

deviation of $26,519. Records indicate 1,445,100 people earn a living in Food Manufacturing.

Removing the top 20% of data appears to eliminate these top-heavy influences and returns the data displayed in Figure 46. Average wage structure value has dropped to $34,264 with a corresponding reduction in standard deviation of $12,292. The Food Manufacturing Johnson Transformation equation is:

$$0.136541 + 0.749292 * Ln((X - 14505.1) / (48712.2 - X)).$$

Evaluating the data range of the lower 80% and the upper 20% shows the upper has more range. There appears inequitable, excessive compensation where the upper 20% of a wage structure has more range than the lower 80% of personnel. In addition, this comparison does not include the more highly paid managers and executives that exceed any of these values. Probability distribution data analysis using the Johnson Transformation results in a P-value of 0.658, confirming a good fit for a normal distribution.

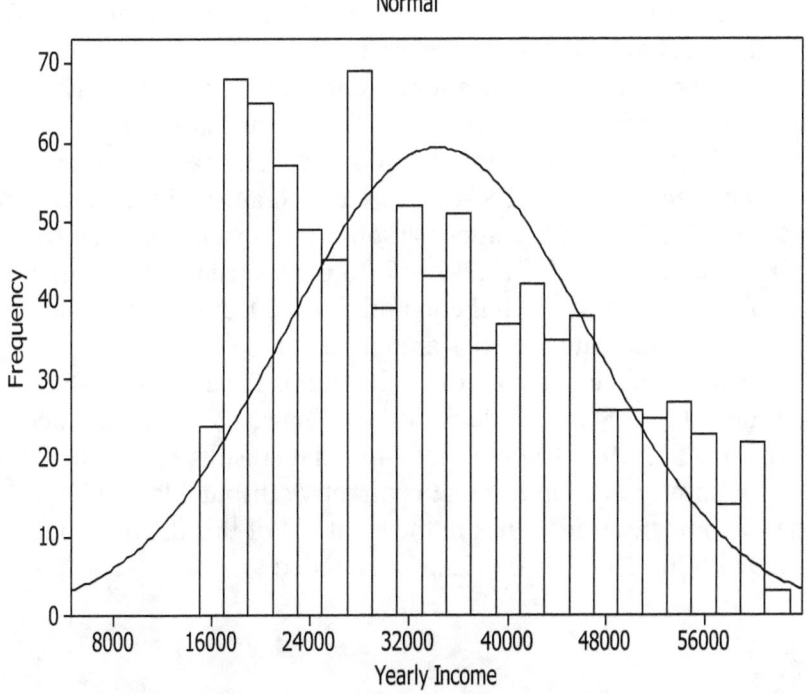

Figure 46. Food Manufacturing Normal Curve

Even if one were to consider Figure 45 a fair representation and the top executive (CEO) salary was limited to $1,000,000, it would require 36 standard deviations to reach the $1,000,000 mark from this larger average: ($1,000,000 - $45,143) / $26,519 = 36.0 standard deviations (rounded).

It is easy to see from observing the charts for Food Manufacturing that each one has a different size scale for the x-axis to represent data. The statistical software automatically calculates scale size and provides an output fitting allowable space on a sheet of paper. Comparison of one figure to another in this fashion can be difficult due to scale differences. However, in an attempt to create an example that is easier to conceptualize, reconsider Figure 6. Figure 6 can be used to compare distances of the mean to any value because it places all standard deviations within a uniform distance on its scale. Regardless of standard deviation amount, it takes only one inch of space across the scale. Three standard deviations from the average represent approximately 99.865% of the lower 80% of a workforce. The further we move right, the more rare an individual becomes with a truly unique ability of 1/1,000,000 workers represented at 4.75 (inches) standard deviations. With Figure 45, the CEOs salary is over 3 <u>feet</u> away from the average.

We considered the case for all data in Figure 45 with its resulting 36 standard deviations and 3 feet distance to reach $1,000,000, let us now consider the more realistic case of Figure 46. Using the revised values of $34,264 as an average and standard deviation of $12,292, the compensation gap overruns the ruler to ($1,000,000 - $34,264) / $12,292 = 78.6 inches (rounded), or more than 6 feet 6 inches to reach the hypothetical CEO's salary, much more if reality indicates salaries are larger for executives.

Another factor worthy of evaluation is the change in standard deviation values. Standard deviation for Figure 45 is $26,519 and Figure 46 is $12,292. Using Figure 46's data results in over a 53% reduction in wage variability that is directly attributable to a large range of compensation values in the right tail of this distribution: (1 - ($12,292 / $26,519)) * 100 = 53.3% (rounded).

Fabricated Metal Product Manufacturing

Many processes are involved in the Fabricated Metal Product Manufacturing industries that include forging, stamping, bending, forming, and machining that render metallic materials into intermediate or final end products. Common products include cutlery, hardware items, springs, wire, hand tools, and creation of boilers, tanks, and shipping containers. Occupations include various machine operators and tenders, machinists, welders and managers

Using the data within the Fabricated Metal Product Manufacturing industries resulted in a histogram with a long tail to the right as displayed in Figure 47. More bars on the right side that decrease in value than on the left indicate a positively skewed distribution. There are irregular gaps in the right tail.

Remember the dice example where a large number skewed the mean and standard deviation results? We can easily see there are large values in the tail of Figure 47. Using a statistical program to evaluate all data resulted in an average of $48,781 and standard

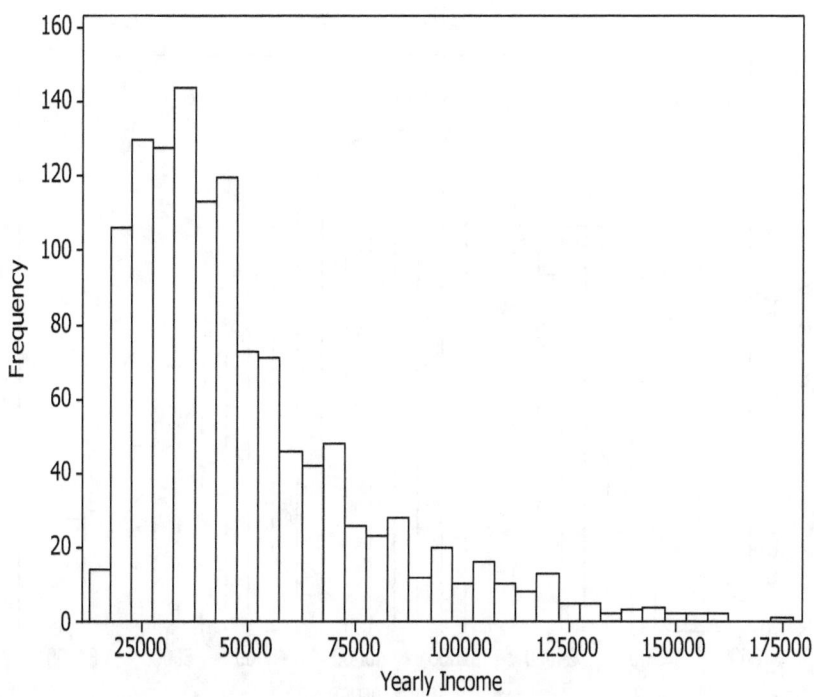

Figure 47. Fabricated Metal Product Manufacturing Wage Structure

deviation of $26,675. Records indicate 1,264,990 people earn a living in Fabricated Metal Product Manufacturing.

Removing the top 20% of data appears to eliminate these top-heavy influences and returns the data displayed in Figure 48. Average wage structure value has dropped to $37,830 with a corresponding reduction in standard deviation of $12,672. The Fabricated Metal Product Manufacturing Johnson Transformation equation is:

$$0.366976 + 0.816675 * Ln((X - 14916.7) \ / (66932.7 - X)).$$

Evaluating the data range of the lower 80% and the upper 20% shows the upper has more range. There appears inequitable, excessive compensation where the upper 20% of a wage structure has more range than the lower 80% of personnel. In addition, this comparison does not include the more highly paid managers and executives that exceed any of these values. Probability distribution data analysis using the Johnson Transformation results in a P-value

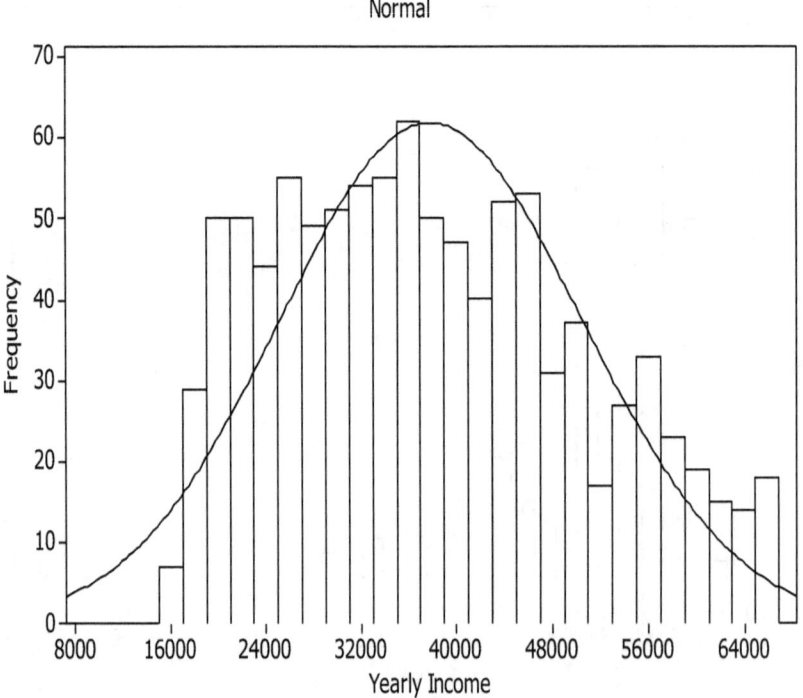

Figure 48. Fabricated Metal Product Manufacturing Normal Curve

of 0.459, confirming a good fit for a normal distribution.

Even if one were to consider Figure 47 a fair representation and the top executive (CEO) salary was limited to $1,000,000, it would require over 35 standard deviations to reach the $1,000,000 mark from this larger average: ($1,000,000 - $48,781) / $26,675 = 35.7 standard deviations (rounded).

It is easy to see from observing the charts for Fabricated Metal Product Manufacturing that each one has a different size scale for the x-axis to represent data. The statistical software automatically calculates scale size and provides an output fitting allowable space on a sheet of paper. Comparison of one figure to another in this fashion can be difficult due to scale differences. However, in an attempt to create an example that is easier to conceptualize, reconsider Figure 6. Figure 6 can be used to compare distances of the mean to any value because it places all standard deviations within a uniform distance on its scale. Regardless of standard deviation amount, it takes only one inch of space across the scale. Three standard deviations from the average represent approximately 99.865% of the lower 80% of a workforce. The further we move right, the more rare an individual becomes with a truly unique ability of 1/1,000,000 workers represented at 4.75 (inches) standard deviations. With Figure 47, the CEOs salary is almost 3 <u>feet</u> away from the average.

We considered the case for all data in Figure 47 with its resulting 35 standard deviations and 3 feet distance to reach $1,000,000, let us now consider the more realistic case of Figure 48. Using the revised values of $37,830 as an average and standard deviation of $12,672, the compensation gap overruns the ruler to ($1,000,000 - $37,830) / $12,672 = 75.9 inches (rounded), or approximately 6 feet 4 inches to reach the hypothetical CEO's salary, much more if reality indicates salaries are larger for executives.

Another factor worthy of evaluation is the change in standard deviation values. Standard deviation for Figure 47 is $26,675 and Figure 48 is $12,672. Using Figure 48's data results in over a 52% reduction in wage variability that is directly attributable to a large range of compensation values in the right tail of this distribution: (1 - ($12,672 / $26,675)) * 100 = 52.5% (rounded).

Transportation Equipment Manufacturing

These industries focus on equipment production involved in transportation of people and products. Many common processes involved in other industries are present: bending, forming, welding, machining, and assembly operations that incorporate assembly of components into subassemblies that result in finished vehicles, railroad rolling stock, ships and boats, and trailers. Aerospace and mechanical engineers, machinists, and welders are some occupations.

Using the data within the Transportation Equipment Manufacturing industries resulted in a histogram with a long tail to the right as displayed in Figure 49. More bars on the right side that decrease in value than on the left indicate a positively skewed distribution. There are irregular gaps in the right tail.

Remember the dice example where a large number skewed the mean and standard deviation results? We can easily see there are large values in the tail of Figure 49. Using a statistical program to evaluate all data resulted in an average of $54,317 and standard

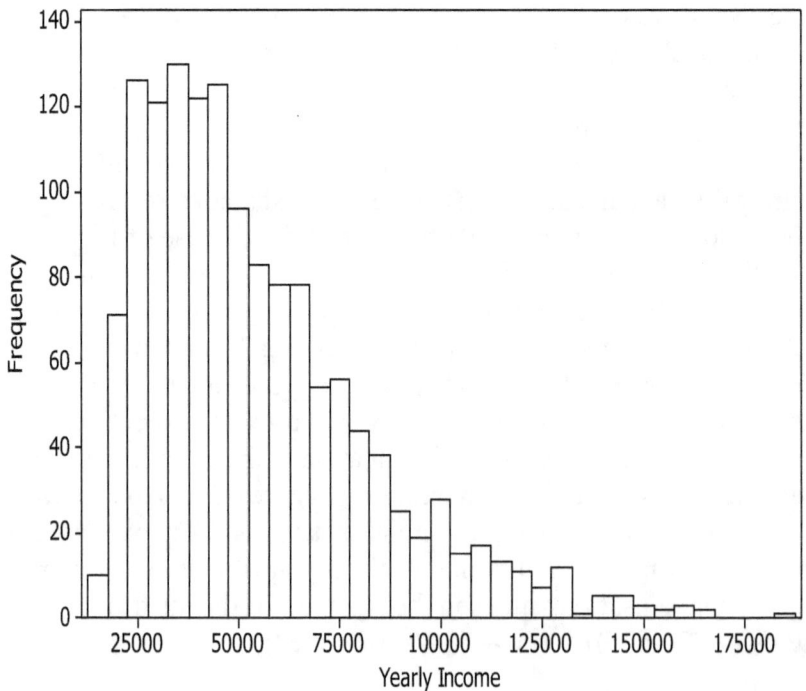

Figure 49. Transportation Equipment Manufacturing Wage Structure

deviation of $27,979. Records indicate 1,329,370 people earn a living in Transportation Equipment Manufacturing.

Removing the top 20% of data appears to eliminate these top-heavy influences and returns the data displayed in Figure 50. Average wage structure value has dropped to $43,088 with a corresponding reduction in standard deviation of $15,177. The Transportation Equipment Manufacturing Johnson Transformation equation is:

$$0.503715 + 0.952512 * Ln((X - 14273.2) / (64194.6 - X)).$$

Evaluating the data range of the lower 80% and the upper 20% shows the upper has more range. There appears inequitable, excessive compensation where the upper 20% of a wage structure has more range than the lower 80% of personnel. In addition, this comparison does not include the more highly paid managers and executives that exceed any of these values. Probability distribution data analysis using the Johnson Transformation results in a P-value

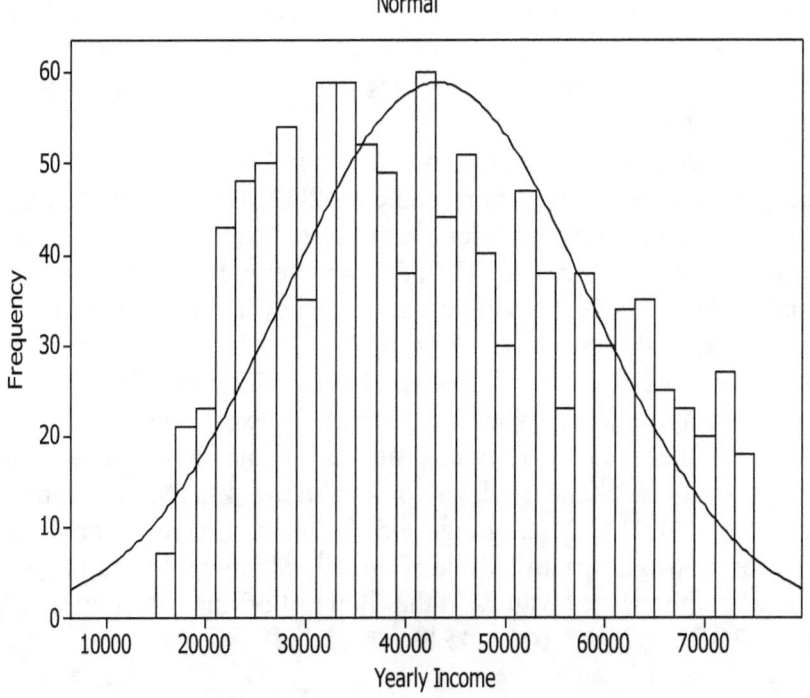

Figure 50. Transportation Equipment Manufacturing Normal Curve

of 0.123, confirming a good fit for a normal distribution.

Even if one were to consider Figure 49 a fair representation and the top executive (CEO) salary was limited to $1,000,000, it would require over 33 standard deviations to reach the $1,000,000 mark from this larger average: ($1,000,000 - $54,317) / $27,979 = 33.8 standard deviations (rounded).

It is easy to see from observing the charts for Transportation Equipment Manufacturing that each one has a different size scale for the x-axis to represent data. The statistical software automatically calculates scale size and provides an output fitting allowable space on a sheet of paper. Comparison of one figure to another in this fashion can be difficult due to scale differences. However, in an attempt to create an example that is easier to conceptualize, reconsider Figure 6. Figure 6 can be used to compare distances of the mean to any value because it places all standard deviations within a uniform distance on its scale. Regardless of standard deviation amount, it takes only one inch of space across the scale. Three standard deviations from the average represent approximately 99.865% of the lower 80% of a workforce. The further we move right, the more rare an individual becomes with a truly unique ability of 1/1,000,000 workers represented at 4.75 (inches) standard deviations. With Figure 49, the CEOs salary is over 2 feet 8 inches away from the average.

We considered the case for all data in Figure 49 with its resulting 33 standard deviations and over 2-1/2 feet distance to reach $1,000,000, let us now consider the more realistic case of Figure 50. Using the revised values of $43,088 as an average and standard deviation of $15,177, the compensation gap overruns the ruler to ($1,000,000 - $43,088) / $15,177 = 63.1 inches (rounded), or more than 5 feet 3 inches to reach the hypothetical CEO's salary, much more if reality indicates salaries are larger for executives.

Another factor worthy of evaluation is the change in standard deviation values. Standard deviation for Figure 49 is $27,979 and Figure 50 is $15,177. Using Figure 50's data results in over a 45% reduction in wage variability that is directly attributable to a large range of compensation values in the right tail of this distribution: (1 - ($15,177 / $27,979)) * 100 = 45.8% (rounded).

Durable Goods Merchant Wholesalers

These industries are involved with the sale of capital or durable goods to other businesses on their own accounts. These items generally involve products with accounting life cycles of three or more years and may involve motor vehicles, machinery and equipment, furniture, sporting goods, spare parts, and major household appliances. Truck drivers, sales representatives, laborers, and shipping and receiving clerks are some frequent occupations.

Using the data within the Durable Goods Merchant Wholesalers industries resulted in a histogram with a long tail to the right as displayed in Figure 51. More bars on the right side that decrease in value than on the left indicate a positively skewed distribution. There are irregular gaps in the right tail.

Remember the dice example where a large number skewed the mean and standard deviation results? We can easily see there are large values in the tail of Figure 51. Using a statistical program to evaluate all data resulted in an average of $47,491 and standard

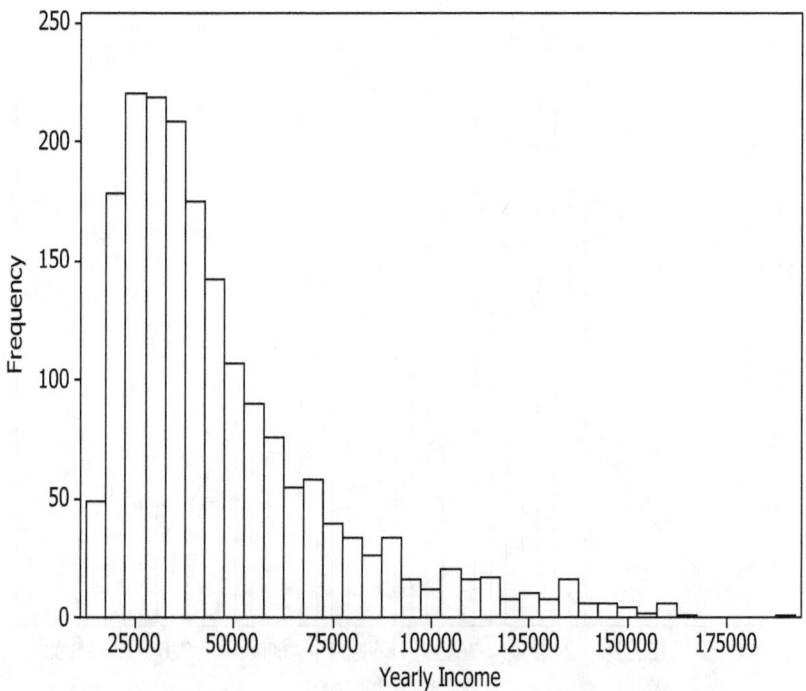

Figure 51. Merchant Wholesalers, Durable Goods Wage Structure

deviation of $28,075. Records indicate 2,715,310 people earn a living in Durable Goods Merchant Wholesalers.

Removing the top 20% of data appears to eliminate these top-heavy influences and returns the data displayed in Figure 52. Average wage structure value has dropped to $40,498 with a corresponding reduction in standard deviation of $17,289. The Durable Goods Merchant Wholesalers Johnson Transformation equation is:

$$0.491426 + 0.722278 * Ln((X - 15241.0) / (55928.4 - X)).$$

Evaluating the data range of the lower 80% and the upper 20% shows the upper has more range. There appears inequitable, excessive compensation where the upper 20% of a wage structure has more range than the lower 80% of personnel. In addition, this comparison does not include the more highly paid managers and executives that exceed any of these values. Probability distribution data analysis using the Johnson Transformation results in a P-value

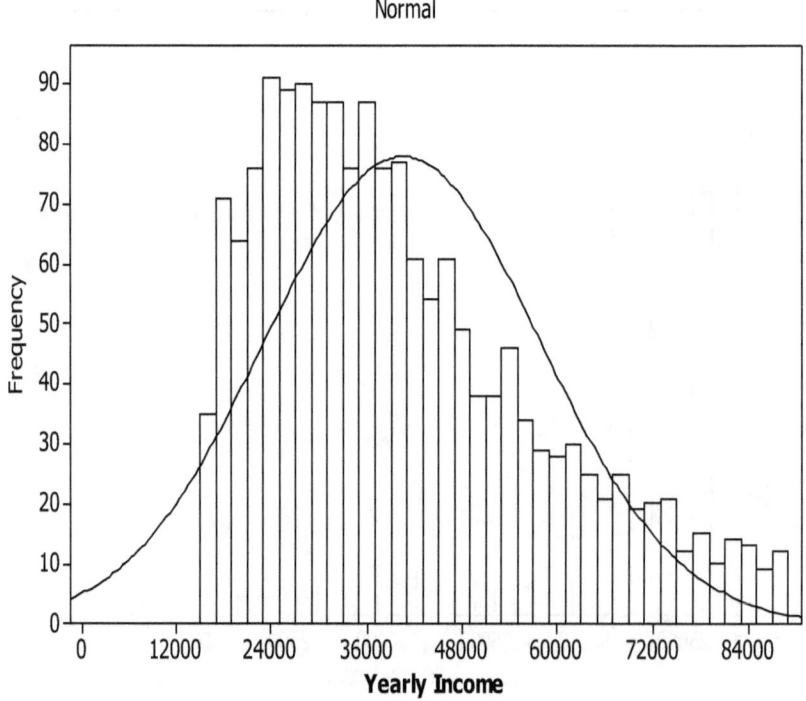

Figure 52. Durable Goods Merchant Wholesalers Normal Curve

of 0.230, confirming a good fit for a normal distribution.

Even if one were to consider Figure 51 a fair representation and the top executive (CEO) salary was limited to $1,000,000, it would require over 33 standard deviations to reach the $1,000,000 mark from this larger average: ($1,000,000 - $47,491) / $28,075 = 33.9 standard deviations (rounded).

It is easy to see from observing the charts for Durable Goods Merchant Wholesalers that each one has a different size scale for the x-axis to represent data. The statistical software automatically calculates scale size and provides an output fitting allowable space on a sheet of paper. Comparison of one figure to another in this fashion can be difficult due to scale differences. However, in an attempt to create an example that is easier to conceptualize, reconsider Figure 6. Figure 6 can be used to compare distances of the mean to any value because it places all standard deviations within a uniform distance on its scale. Regardless of standard deviation amount, it takes only one inch of space across the scale. Three standard deviations from the average represent approximately 99.865% of the lower 80% of a workforce. The further we move right, the more rare an individual becomes with a truly unique ability of 1/1,000,000 workers represented at 4.75 (inches) standard deviations. With Figure 51, the CEOs salary is well over 2-1/2 <u>feet</u> away from the average.

We considered the case for all data in Figure 51 with its resulting 33 standard deviations and 2-1/2 feet distance to reach $1,000,000, let us now consider the more realistic case of Figure 52. Using the revised values of $40,498 as an average and standard deviation of $17,289, the compensation gap overruns the ruler to ($1,000,000 - $40,498) / $17,289 = 55.5 inches (rounded), or more than 4 feet 7 inches to reach the hypothetical CEO's salary, much more if reality indicates salaries are larger for executives.

Another factor worthy of evaluation is the change in standard deviation values. Standard deviation for Figure 51 is $28,075 and Figure 52 is $17,289. Using Figure 52's data results in over a 38% reduction in wage variability that is directly attributable to a large range of compensation values in the right tail of this distribution: (1 - ($17,289 / $28,075)) * 100 = 38.4% (rounded).

Nondurable Goods Merchant Wholesalers

These industries are involved in the wholesale of products that have an accounting life cycle of less than three years to other businesses. Among these products are paper and paper products, chemicals and chemical products, drugs, textiles, apparel, footwear, groceries, alcoholic beverages, books, magazines, flowers and nursery stock, farm products, and tobacco products. Frequent employment occupations include laborers, truck drivers, etc.

Using the data within the Nondurable Goods Merchant Wholesalers (NGMW) industries resulted in a histogram with a long tail to the right as displayed in Figure 53. More bars on the right side that decrease in value than on the left indicate a positively skewed distribution. There are irregular gaps in the right tail.

Remember the dice example where a large number skewed the mean and standard deviation results? We can easily see there are large values in the tail of Figure 53. Using a statistical program to evaluate all data resulted in an average of $48,195 and standard

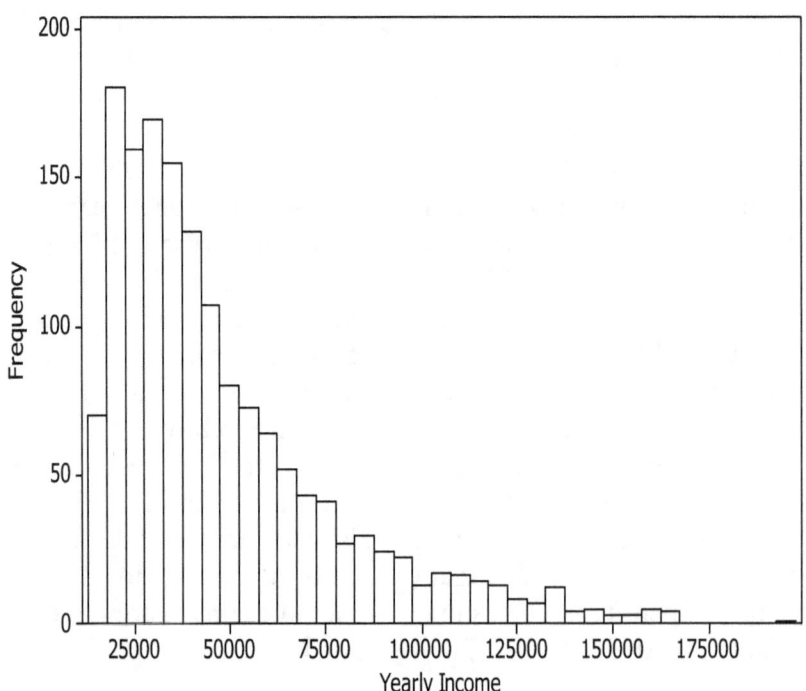

Figure 53. NGMW Wage Structure

deviation of $29,782. Records indicate 1,953,670 people earn a living in NGMW.

Removing the top 20% of data appears to eliminate these top-heavy influences and returns the data displayed in Figure 54. Average wage structure value has dropped to $35,,847 with a corresponding reduction in standard deviation of $13,686. The NGMW Johnson Transformation equation is:

$$0.531343 + 0.763274 * Ln((X - 14538.5) / (70929.2 - X)).$$

Evaluating the data range of the lower 80% and the upper 20% shows the upper has more range. There appears inequitable, excessive compensation where the upper 20% of a wage structure has more range than the lower 80% of personnel. In addition, this comparison does not include the more highly paid managers and executives that exceed any of these values. Probability distribution data analysis using the Johnson Transformation results in a P-value of 0.127, confirming a good fit for a normal distribution.

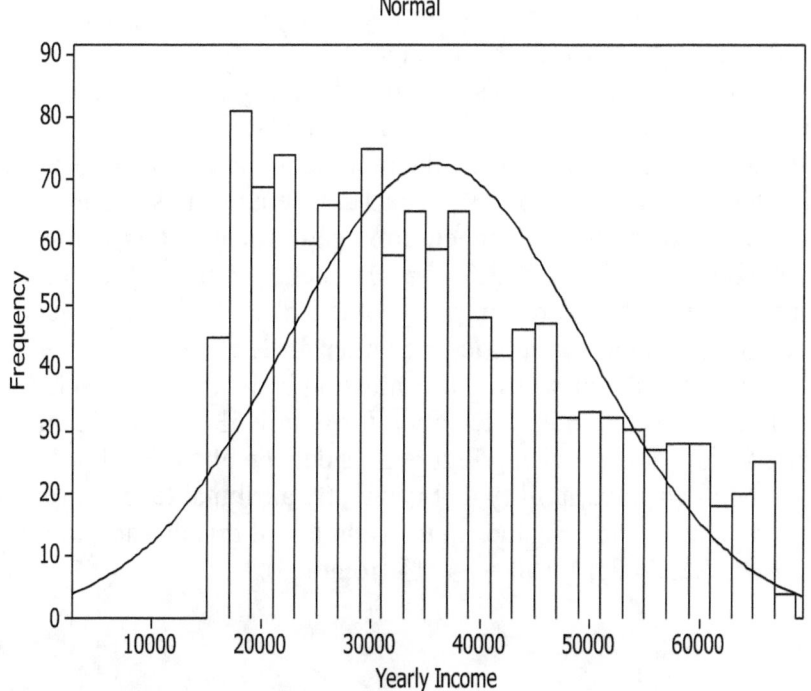

Figure 54. NGMW Normal Curve

Even if one were to consider Figure 53 a fair representation and the top executive (CEO) salary was limited to $1,000,000, it would require over 32 standard deviations to reach the $1,000,000 mark from this larger average: ($1,000,000 - $48,195) / $29,782 = 32.6 standard deviations (rounded).

It is easy to see from observing the charts for NGMW that each one has a different size scale for the x-axis to represent data. The statistical software automatically calculates scale size and provides an output fitting allowable space on a sheet of paper. Comparison of one figure to another in this fashion can be difficult due to scale differences. However, in an attempt to create an example that is easier to conceptualize, reconsider Figure 6. Figure 6 can be used to compare distances of the mean to any value because it places all standard deviations within a uniform distance on its scale. Regardless of standard deviation amount, it takes only one inch of space across the scale. Three standard deviations from the average represent approximately 99.865% of the lower 80% of a workforce. The further we move right, the more rare an individual becomes with a truly unique ability of 1/1,000,000 workers represented at 4.75 (inches) standard deviations. With Figure 53, the CEOs salary is over 2-1/2 <u>feet</u> away from the average.

We considered the case for all data in Figure 53 with its resulting 32 standard deviations and 2-1/2 feet distance to reach $1,000,000, let us now consider the more realistic case of Figure 54. Using the revised values of $35,847 as an average and standard deviation of $13,686, the compensation gap overruns the ruler to ($1,000,000 - $35,847) / $13,686 = 70.4 inches (rounded), or more than 5 feet 10 inches to reach the hypothetical CEO's salary, much more if reality indicates salaries are larger for executives.

Another factor worthy of evaluation is the change in standard deviation values. Standard deviation for Figure 53 is $29,782 and Figure 54 is $13,686. Using Figure 54's data results in a 54% reduction in wage variability that is directly attributable to a large range of compensation values in the right tail of this distribution: (1 - ($13,686 / $29,782)) * 100 = 54.0% (rounded).

Clothing and Clothing Accessories Stores

These industries sell new clothing and clothing accessories at the retail level from established locations to the public. Equipment for product display has similarity in these establishments along with staff members knowledgeable in recent fashion trends and matching of apparel styles, colors, combinations, and accessories in conjunction with customer tastes. Some occupations are cashiers, first line supervisors and managers, salespersons, and tailors.

Using the data within the Clothing and Clothing Accessories Stores industries resulted in a histogram with a long tail to the right as displayed in Figure 55. More bars on the right side that decrease in value than on the left indicate a positively skewed distribution. There are irregular gaps in the right tail.

Remember the dice example where a large number skewed the mean and standard deviation results? We can easily see there are large values in the tail of Figure 55. Using a statistical program to evaluate all data resulted in an average of $41,312 and standard

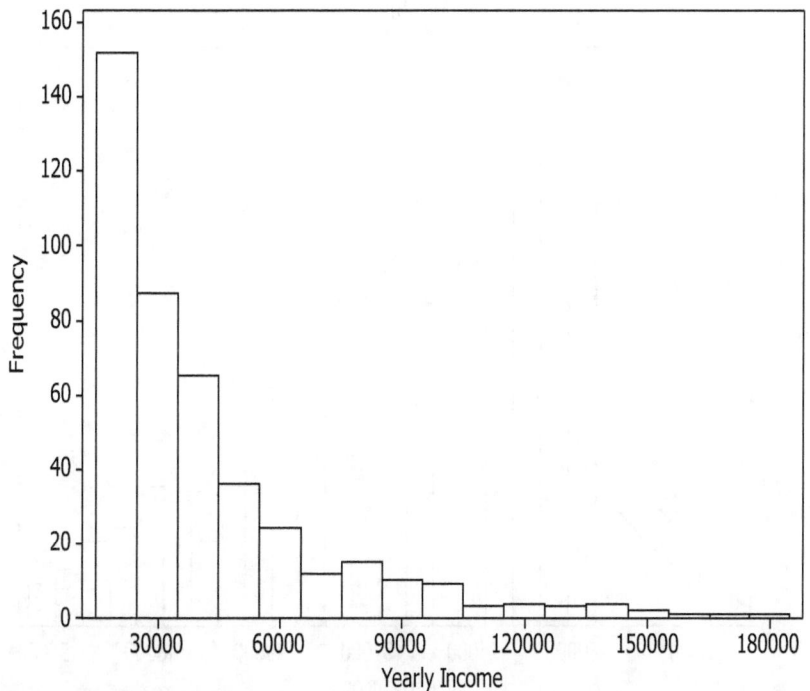

Figure 55. Clothing and Clothing Accessories Stores Wage Structure

deviation of $28,835. Records indicate 1,396,550 people earn a living in Clothing and Clothing Accessories Stores.

Removing the top 20% of data appears to eliminate these top-heavy influences and returns the data displayed in Figure 56. Average wage structure value has dropped to $29,346 with a corresponding reduction in standard deviation of $10,746. The Clothing and Clothing Accessories Stores Johnson Transformation equation is:

$$0.536662 + 0.594565 * Ln((X - 15351.5) / (48045.8 - X)).$$

Evaluating the data range of the lower 80% and the upper 20% shows the upper has more range. There appears inequitable, excessive compensation where the upper 20% of a wage structure has more range than the lower 80% of personnel. In addition, this comparison does not include the more highly paid managers and executives that exceed any of these values. Probability distribution data analysis using the Johnson Transformation results in a P-value

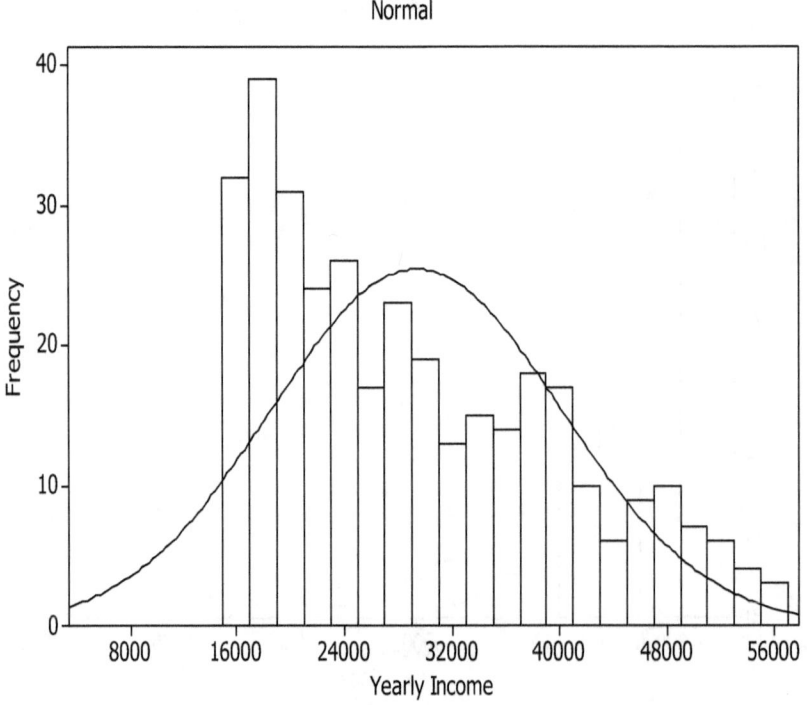

Figure 56. Clothing and Clothing Accessories Stores Normal Curve

of 0.418, confirming a good fit for a normal distribution.

Even if one were to consider Figure 55 a fair representation and the top executive (CEO) salary was limited to $1,000,000, it would require over 33 standard deviations to reach the $1,000,000 mark from this larger average: ($1,000,000 - $41,312) / $28,835 = 33.2 standard deviations (rounded).

It is easy to see from observing the charts for Clothing and Clothing Accessories Stores that each one has a different size scale for the x-axis to represent data. The statistical software automatically calculates scale size and provides an output fitting allowable space on a sheet of paper. Comparison of one figure to another in this fashion can be difficult due to scale differences. However, in an attempt to create an example that is easier to conceptualize, reconsider Figure 6. Figure 6 can be used to compare distances of the mean to any value because it places all standard deviations within a uniform distance on its scale. Regardless of standard deviation amount, it takes only one inch of space across the scale. Three standard deviations from the average represent approximately 99.865% of the lower 80% of a workforce. The further we move right, the more rare an individual becomes with a truly unique ability of 1/1,000,000 workers represented at 4.75 (inches) standard deviations. With Figure 55, the CEOs salary is over 2-1/2 <u>feet</u> away from the average.

We considered the case for all data in Figure 55 with its resulting 33 standard deviations and 2-1/2 feet distance to reach $1,000,000, let us now consider the more realistic case of Figure 56. Using the revised values of $29,346 as an average and standard deviation of $10,746, the compensation gap overruns the ruler to ($1,000,000 - $29,346) / $10,746 = 90.3 inches (rounded), or more than 7 feet 6 inches to reach the hypothetical CEO's salary, much more if reality indicates salaries are larger for executives.

Another factor worthy of evaluation is the change in standard deviation values. Standard deviation for Figure 55 is $28,835 and Figure 56 is $10,746. Using Figure 56's data results in over a 62% reduction in wage variability that is directly attributable to a large range of compensation values in the right tail of this distribution: (1 - ($10,746 / $28,835)) * 100 = 62.7% (rounded).

General Merchandise Stores

These industries are involved in the retail sale of new merchandise from fixed locations. A key characteristic of these establishments is possession of equipment and staff capable of delivering a wide range of products to consumers. Frequently observed occupations include cashiers, customer service representatives, first line supervisors and managers, retail salespersons, and stock clerks.

Using the data within the General Merchandise Stores industries resulted in a histogram with a long tail to the right as displayed in Figure 57. More bars on the right side that decrease in value than on the left indicate a positively skewed distribution. There are irregular gaps in the right tail.

Remember the dice example where a large number skewed the mean and standard deviation results? We can easily see there are large values in the tail of Figure 57. Using a statistical program to evaluate all data resulted in an average of $36,166 and standard

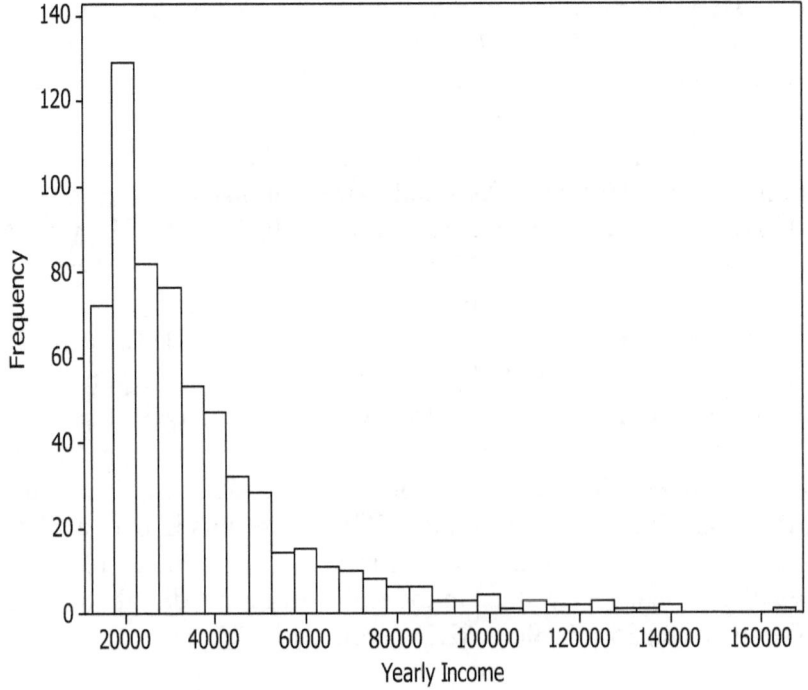

Figure 57. General Merchandise Stores Wage Structure

deviation of $22,901. Records indicate 3,038,350 people earn a living in General Merchandise Stores.

Removing the top 20% of data appears to eliminate these top-heavy influences and returns the data displayed in Figure 58. Average wage structure value has dropped to $26,959 with a corresponding reduction in standard deviation of $8,850. The General Merchandise Stores Johnson Transformation equation is:

$$0.536662 + 0.594565 * Ln((X - 15351.5) / (48045.8 - X)).$$

Evaluating the data range of the lower 80% and the upper 20% shows the upper has more range. There appears inequitable, excessive compensation where the upper 20% of a wage structure has more range than the lower 80% of personnel. In addition, this comparison does not include the more highly paid managers and executives that exceed any of these values. Probability distribution data analysis using the Johnson Transformation results in a P-value of 0.640, confirming a good fit for a normal distribution.

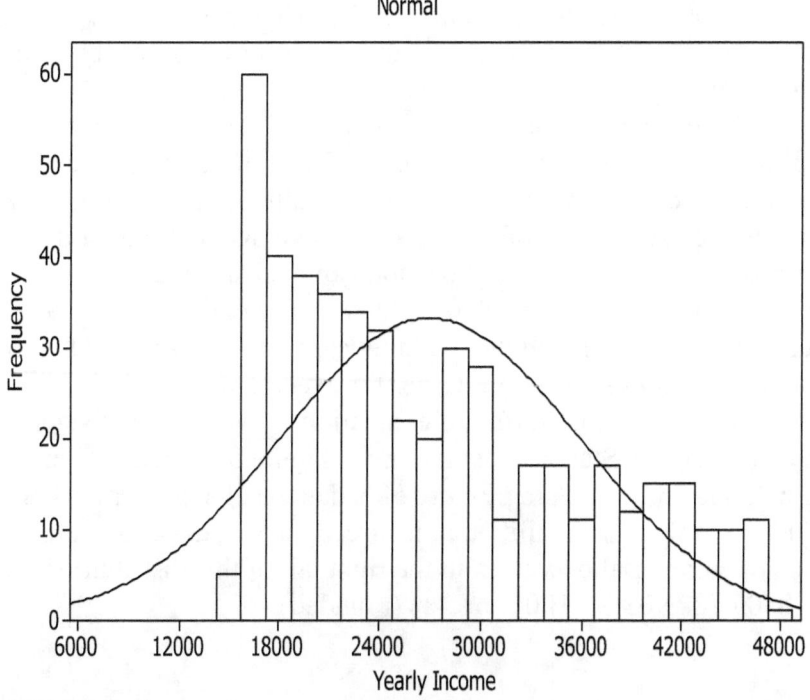

Figure 58. General Merchandise Stores Normal Curve

Even if one were to consider Figure 57 a fair representation and the top executive (CEO) salary was limited to $1,000,000, it would require over 42 standard deviations to reach the $1,000,000 mark from this larger average: ($1,000,000 - $36,166) / $22,901 = 42.1 standard deviations (rounded).

It is easy to see from observing the charts for General Merchandise Stores that each one has a different size scale for the x-axis to represent data. The statistical software automatically calculates scale size and provides an output fitting allowable space on a sheet of paper. Comparison of one figure to another in this fashion can be difficult due to scale differences. However, in an attempt to create an example that is easier to conceptualize, reconsider Figure 6. Figure 6 can be used to compare distances of the mean to any value because it places all standard deviations within a uniform distance on its scale. Regardless of standard deviation amount, it takes only one inch of space across the scale. Three standard deviations from the average represent approximately 99.865% of the lower 80% of a workforce. The further we move right, the more rare an individual becomes with a truly unique ability of 1/1,000,000 workers represented at 4.75 (inches) standard deviations. With Figure 57, the CEOs salary is over 3-1/2 <u>feet</u> away from the average.

We considered the case for all data in Figure 57 with its resulting 42 standard deviations and 3-1/2 feet distance to reach $1,000,000, let us now consider the more realistic case of Figure 58. Using the revised values of $26,959 as an average and standard deviation of $8,850, the compensation gap overruns the ruler to ($1,000,000 - $26,959) / $8,850 = 109.9 inches (rounded), or more than 9 feet 1 inch to reach the hypothetical CEO's salary, much more if reality indicates salaries are larger for executives.

Another factor worthy of evaluation is the change in standard deviation values. Standard deviation for Figure 57 is $22,901 and Figure 58 is $8,850. Using Figure 58's data results in over a 61% reduction in wage variability that is directly attributable to a large range of compensation values in the right tail of this distribution: (1 - ($8,850 / $22,901)) * 100 = 61.4% (rounded).

Truck Transportation

Trucks and tractor trailers are a common means of transporting a wide range of cargo over-the-road in these industries. General and specialized freight transportation are distinguished by equipment, cargo type, scheduling requirements, and terminals utilized. Size, weight, shape, and other requirements dictate unique equipment and ability for specialized movement from one location to another.

Using the data within the Truck Transportation industries resulted in a histogram with a long tail to the right as displayed in Figure 59. More bars on the right side that decrease in value than on the left indicate a positively skewed distribution. There are irregular gaps in the right tail.

Remember the dice example where a large number skewed the mean and standard deviation results? We can easily see there are large values in the tail of Figure 59. Using a statistical program to evaluate all data resulted in an average of $45,657 and standard

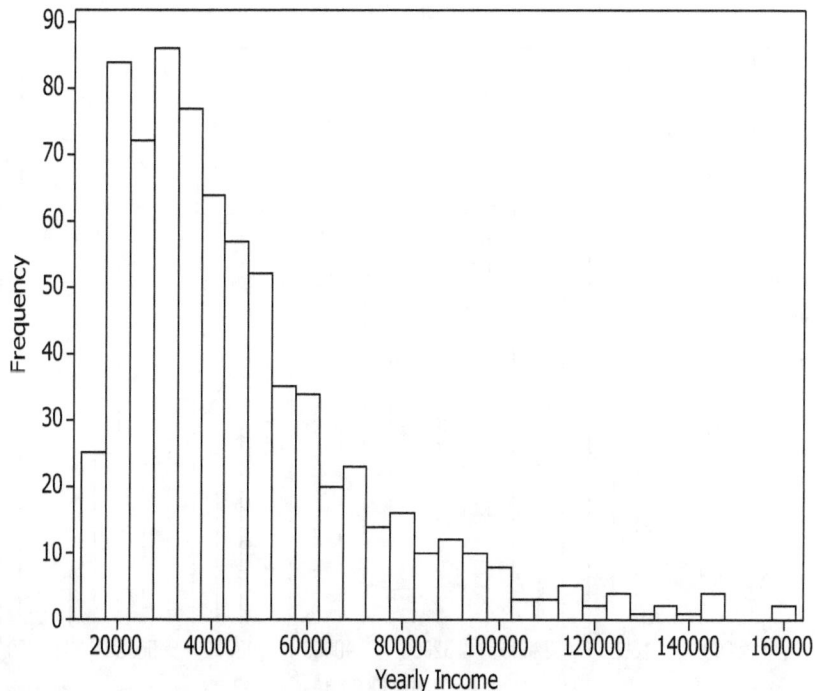

Figure 59. Truck Transportation Wage Structure

deviation of $25,498. Records indicate 1,243,980 people earn a living in Truck Transportation.

Removing the top 20% of data appears to eliminate these top-heavy influences and returns the data displayed in Figure 60. Average wage structure value has dropped to $35,310 with a corresponding reduction in standard deviation of $12,267. The Truck Transportation Johnson Transformation equation is:

$$0.484233 + 0.847427 * Ln((X - 14768.2) / (69998.0 - X)).$$

Evaluating the data range of the lower 80% and the upper 20% shows the upper has more range. There appears inequitable, excessive compensation where the upper 20% of a wage structure has more range than the lower 80% of personnel. In addition, this comparison does not include the more highly paid managers and executives that exceed any of these values. Probability distribution data analysis using the Johnson Transformation results in a P-value of 0.579, confirming a good fit for a normal distribution.

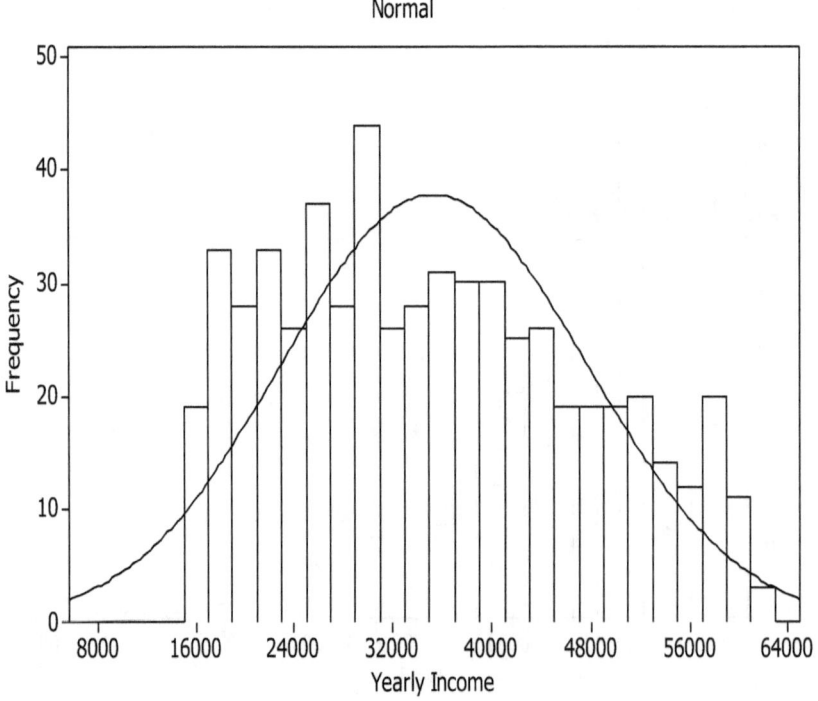

Figure 60. Truck Transportation Normal Curve

Even if one were to consider Figure 59 a fair representation and the top executive (CEO) salary was limited to $1,000,000, it would require over 37 standard deviations to reach the $1,000,000 mark from this larger average: ($1,000,000 - $45,657) / $25,498 = 37.4 standard deviations (rounded).

It is easy to see from observing the charts for Truck Transportation that each one has a different size scale for the x-axis to represent data. The statistical software automatically calculates scale size and provides an output fitting allowable space on a sheet of paper. Comparison of one figure to another in this fashion can be difficult due to scale differences. However, in an attempt to create an example that is easier to conceptualize, reconsider Figure 6. Figure 6 can be used to compare distances of the mean to any value because it places all standard deviations within a uniform distance on its scale. Regardless of standard deviation amount, it takes only one inch of space across the scale. Three standard deviations from the average represent approximately 99.865% of the lower 80% of a workforce. The further we move right, the more rare an individual becomes with a truly unique ability of 1/1,000,000 workers represented at 4.75 (inches) standard deviations. With Figure 59, the CEOs salary is over 3 <u>feet</u> away from the average.

We considered the case for all data in Figure 59 with its resulting 37 standard deviations and 3 feet distance to reach $1,000,000, let us now consider the more realistic case of Figure 60. Using the revised values of $35,310 as an average and standard deviation of $12,267, the compensation gap overruns the ruler to ($1,000,000 - $35,310) / $12,267 = 78.6 inches (rounded), or more than 6 feet 6 inches to reach the hypothetical CEO's salary, much more if reality indicates salaries are larger for executives.

Another factor worthy of evaluation is the change in standard deviation values. Standard deviation for Figure 59 is $25,498 and Figure 60 is $12,267. Using Figure 60's data results in over a 51% reduction in wage variability that is directly attributable to a large range of compensation values in the right tail of this distribution: (1 - ($12,267 / $25,498)) * 100 = 51.9% (rounded).

Nursing and Residential Care Facilities

Residential care with focus on providing services related to nursing, supervision, or other specialized care as needed by residents is the focus of this industry. Facilities are key in providing the processes and care needed for consumers and can include a mix of health and social services applications. Nursing services at some level are frequently and integral part of these activities. Practical and vocational nurses, aids, orderlies, and RNs are frequent occupations.

Using the data within the Nursing and Residential Care Facilities industries resulted in a histogram with a long tail to the right as displayed in Figure 61. More bars on the right side that decrease in value than on the left indicate a positively skewed distribution. There are irregular gaps in the right tail.

Remember the dice example where a large number skewed the mean and standard deviation results? We can easily see there are large values in the tail of Figure 61. Using a statistical program to evaluate all data resulted in an average of $42,360 and standard

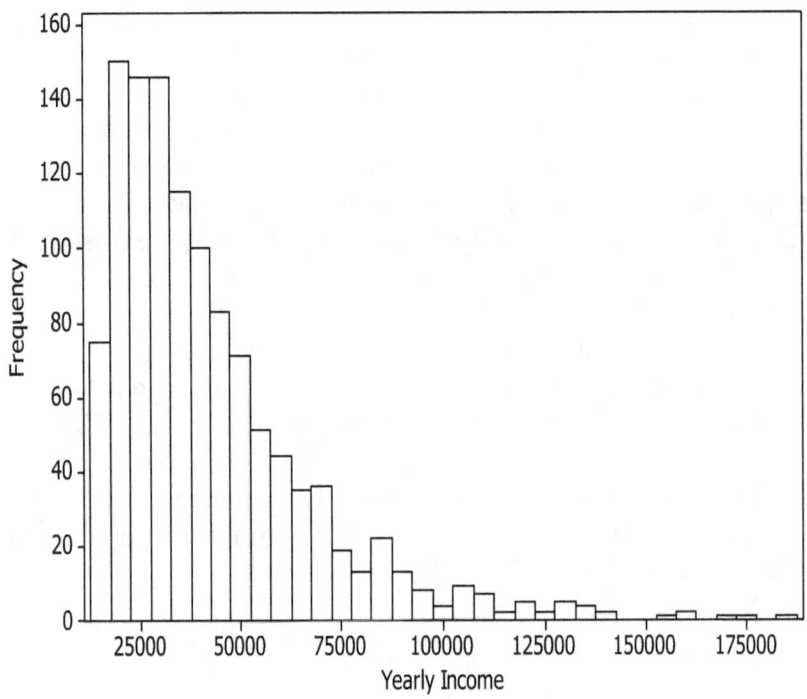

Figure 61. Nursing and Residential Care Facilities Wage Structure

deviation of $24,843. Records indicate 3,122,980 people earn a living in Nursing and Residential Care Facilities.

Removing the top 20% of data appears to eliminate these top-heavy influences and returns the data displayed in Figure 62. Average wage structure value has dropped to $32,401 with a corresponding reduction in standard deviation of $11,270. The Nursing and Residential Care Facilities Johnson Transformation equation is:

$$0.421659 + 0.716937 * Ln((X - 14866.1) / (59398.7 - X)).$$

Evaluating the data range of the lower 80% and the upper 20% shows the upper has more range. There appears inequitable, excessive compensation where the upper 20% of a wage structure has more range than the lower 80% of personnel. In addition, this comparison does not include the more highly paid managers and executives that exceed any of these values. Probability distribution data analysis using the Johnson Transformation results in a P-value

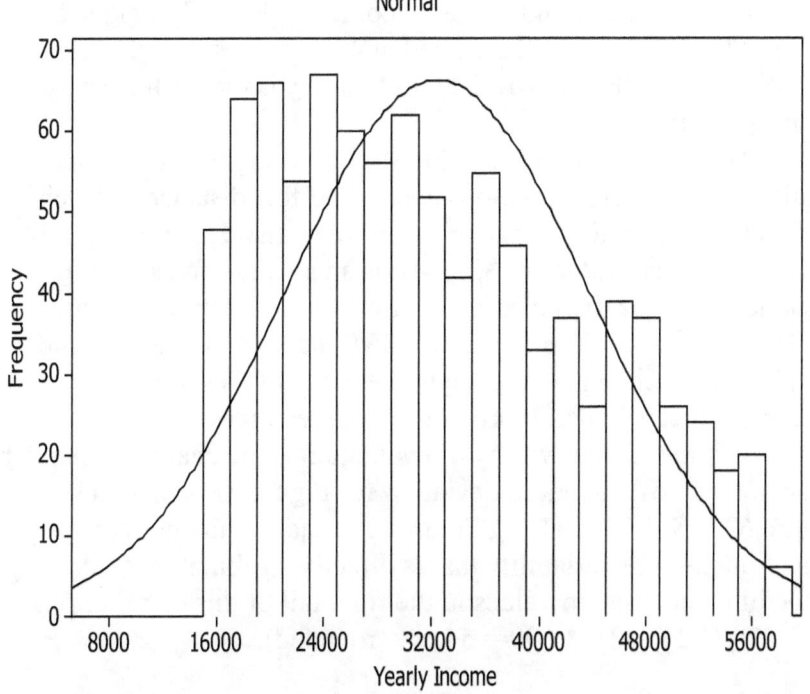

Figure 62. Nursing and Residential Care Facilities Normal Curve

of 0.271, confirming a good fit for a normal distribution.

Even if one were to consider Figure 61 a fair representation and the top executive (CEO) salary was limited to $1,000,000, it would require over 38 standard deviations to reach the $1,000,000 mark from this larger average: ($1,000,000 - $42,360) / $24,843 = 38.5 standard deviations (rounded).

It is easy to see from observing the charts for Nursing and Residential Care Facilities that each one has a different size scale for the x-axis to represent data. The statistical software automatically calculates scale size and provides an output fitting allowable space on a sheet of paper. Comparison of one figure to another in this fashion can be difficult due to scale differences. However, in an attempt to create an example that is easier to conceptualize, reconsider Figure 6. Figure 6 can be used to compare distances of the mean to any value because it places all standard deviations within a uniform distance on its scale. Regardless of standard deviation amount, it takes only one inch of space across the scale. Three standard deviations from the average represent approximately 99.865% of the lower 80% of a workforce. The further we move right, the more rare an individual becomes with a truly unique ability of 1/1,000,000 workers represented at 4.75 (inches) standard deviations. With Figure 61, the CEOs salary is over 3 _feet_ away from the average.

We considered the case for all data in Figure 61 with its resulting 38 standard deviations and over 3 feet distance to reach $1,000,000, let us now consider the more realistic case of Figure 62. Using the revised values of $32,401 as an average and standard deviation of $11,270, the compensation gap overruns the ruler to ($1,000,000 - $32,401) / $11,270 = 85.9 inches (rounded), or more than 7 feet 1 inch to reach the hypothetical CEO's salary, much more if reality indicates salaries are larger for executives.

Another factor worthy of evaluation is the change in standard deviation values. Standard deviation for Figure 61 is $24,843 and Figure 62 is $11,270. Using Figure 62's data results in over a 54% reduction in wage variability that is directly attributable to a large range of compensation values in the right tail of this distribution: (1 - ($11,270 / $24,843)) * 100 = 54.6% (rounded).

Food Services and Drinking Places

Preparation of meals, snack items, and beverages for immediate on- and off-premises consumption according to customer orders is the focus of these industries. The range of amenities varies by establishment from only food and drink to a range of seating accommodations, server services, entertainment, catering, and delivery. Occupations include food preparers, cooks, first line supervisors and managers, and servers.

Using the data within the Food Services and Drinking Places industries resulted in a histogram with a long tail to the right as displayed in Figure 63. More bars on the right side that decrease in value than on the left indicate a positively skewed distribution. There are irregular gaps in the right tail.

Remember the dice example where a large number skewed the mean and standard deviation results? We can easily see there are large values in the tail of Figure 63. Using a statistical program to evaluate all data resulted in an average of $35,628 and standard

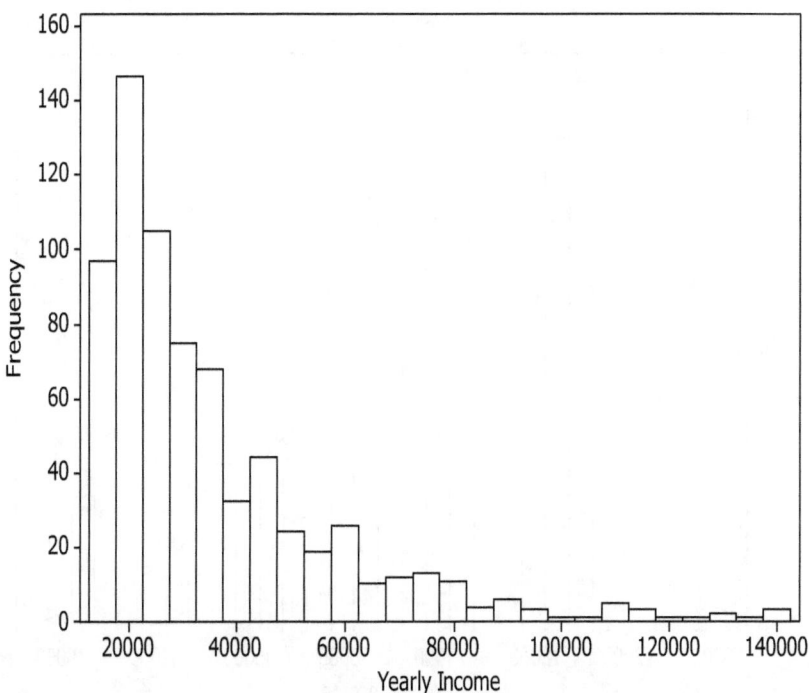

Figure 63. Food Services and Drinking Places Wage Structure

deviation of $22,311. Records indicate 9,376,990 people earn a living in Food Services and Drinking Places.

Removing the top 20% of data appears to eliminate these top-heavy influences and returns the data displayed in Figure 64. Average wage structure value has dropped to $26,467 with a corresponding reduction in standard deviation of $9,108. The Food Services and Drinking Places Johnson Transformation equation is:

$$0.693921 + 0.603102 * Ln((X - 15339.6) / (49628.0 - X)).$$

Evaluating the data range of the lower 80% and the upper 20% shows the upper has more range. There appears inequitable, excessive compensation where the upper 20% of a wage structure has more range than the lower 80% of personnel. In addition, this comparison does not include the more highly paid managers and executives that exceed any of these values. Probability distribution data analysis using the Johnson Transformation results in a P-value of 0.714, confirming a good fit for a normal distribution.

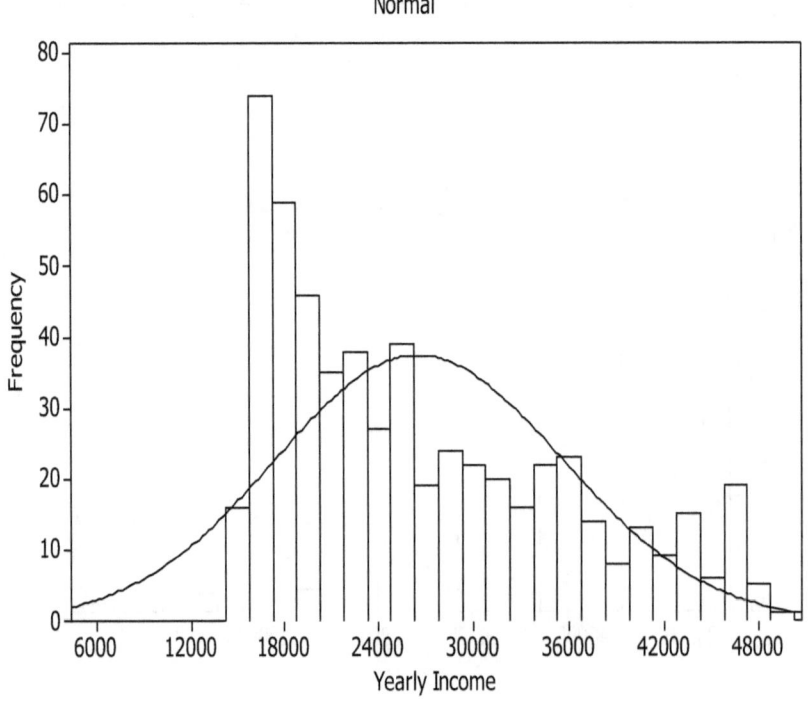

Figure 64. Food Services and Drinking Places Normal Curve

Even if one were to consider Figure 63 a fair representation and the top executive (CEO) salary was limited to $1,000,000, it would require over 43 standard deviations to reach the $1,000,000 mark from this larger average: ($1,000,000 - $35,628) / $22,311 = 43.2 standard deviations (rounded).

It is easy to see from observing the charts for Food Services and Drinking Places that each one has a different size scale for the x-axis to represent data. The statistical software automatically calculates scale size and provides an output fitting allowable space on a sheet of paper. Comparison of one figure to another in this fashion can be difficult due to scale differences. However, in an attempt to create an example that is easier to conceptualize, reconsider Figure 6. Figure 6 can be used to compare distances of the mean to any value because it places all standard deviations within a uniform distance on its scale. Regardless of standard deviation amount, it takes only one inch of space across the scale. Three standard deviations from the average represent approximately 99.865% of the lower 80% of a workforce. The further we move right, the more rare an individual becomes with a truly unique ability of 1/1,000,000 workers represented at 4.75 (inches) standard deviations. With Figure 63, the CEOs salary is over 3-1/2 <u>feet</u> away from the average.

We considered the case for all data in Figure 63 with its resulting 43 standard deviations and 3-1/2 feet distance to reach $1,000,000, let us now consider the more realistic case of Figure 64. Using the revised values of $26,467 as an average and standard deviation of $9,108, the compensation gap overruns the ruler to ($1,000,000 - $26,467) / $9,108 = 106.9 inches (rounded), or more than 8 feet 10 inches to reach the hypothetical CEO's salary, much more if reality indicates salaries are larger for executives.

Another factor worthy of evaluation is the change in standard deviation values. Standard deviation for Figure 63 is $22,311 and Figure 64 is $9,108. Using Figure 64's data results in over a 59% reduction in wage variability that is directly attributable to a large range of compensation values in the right tail of this distribution: (1 - ($9,108 / $22,311)) * 100 = 59.2% (rounded).

Repair and Maintenance

Activities in this industry involve the refurbishment and repair of equipment and other items to improved or working order. This may involve performance of routine and preventive maintenance, increasing reliability, and avoidance of production loss through potential breakdowns and unnecessary repairs. Automotive mechanics and body technicians, painters, cleaners, and first line supervisors and manager are some occupations.

Using the data within the Repair and Maintenance industries resulted in a histogram with a long tail to the right as displayed in Figure 65. More bars on the right side that decrease in value than on the left indicate a positively skewed distribution. There are irregular gaps in the right tail.

Remember the dice example where a large number skewed the mean and standard deviation results? We can easily see there are large values in the tail of Figure 65. Using a statistical program to evaluate all data resulted in an average of $44,055 and standard

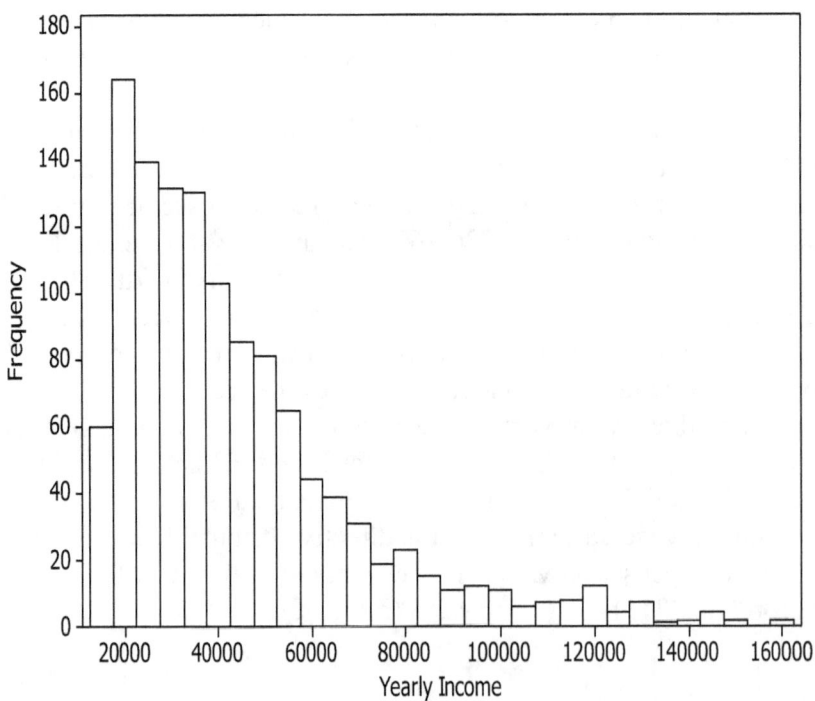

Figure 94. Repair and Maintenance Wage Structure

deviation of $25,827. Records indicate 1,137,690 people earn a living in Repair and Maintenance.

Removing the top 20% of data appears to eliminate these top-heavy influences and returns the data displayed in Figure 66. Average wage structure value has dropped to $33,580 with a corresponding reduction in standard deviation of $11,986. The Repair and Maintenance Johnson Transformation equation is:

$$0.385640 + 0.687939 * Ln((X - 15217.8) / (60671.2 - X)).$$

Evaluating the data range of the lower 80% and the upper 20% shows the upper has more range. There appears inequitable, excessive compensation where the upper 20% of a wage structure has more range than the lower 80% of personnel. In addition, this comparison does not include the more highly paid managers and executives that exceed any of these values. Probability distribution data analysis using the Johnson Transformation results in a P-value of 0.416, confirming a good fit for a normal distribution.

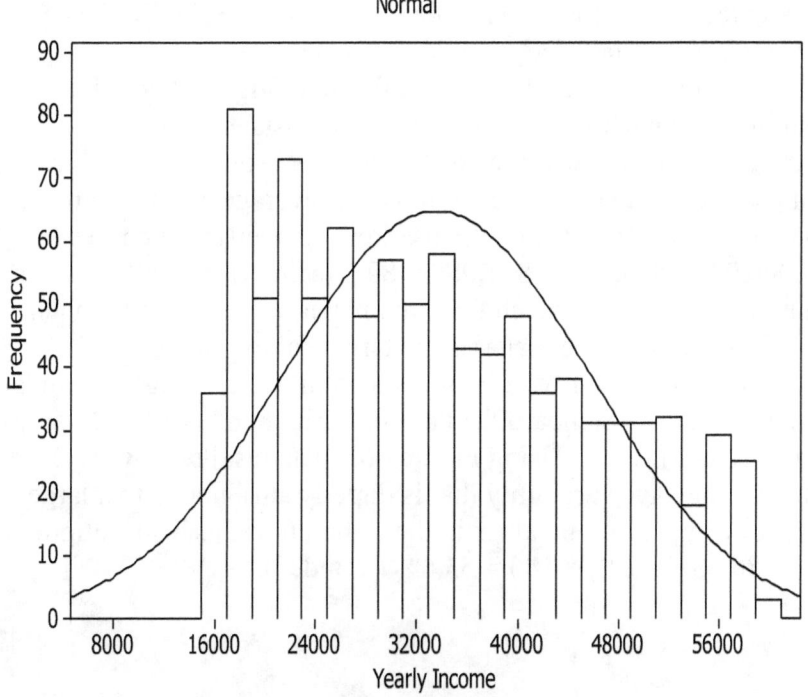

Figure 66. Repair and Maintenance Normal Curve

Even if one were to consider Figure 65 a fair representation and the top executive (CEO) salary was limited to $1,000,000, it would require 37 standard deviations to reach the $1,000,000 mark from this larger average: ($1,000,000 - $44,055) / $25,827 = 37.0 standard deviations (rounded).

It is easy to see from observing the charts for Repair and Maintenance that each one has a different size scale for the x-axis to represent data. The statistical software automatically calculates scale size and provides an output fitting allowable space on a sheet of paper. Comparison of one figure to another in this fashion can be difficult due to scale differences. However, in an attempt to create an example that is easier to conceptualize, reconsider Figure 6. Figure 6 can be used to compare distances of the mean to any value because it places all standard deviations within a uniform distance on its scale. Regardless of standard deviation amount, it takes only one inch of space across the scale. Three standard deviations from the average represent approximately 99.865% of the lower 80% of a workforce. The further we move right, the more rare an individual becomes with a truly unique ability of 1/1,000,000 workers represented at 4.75 (inches) standard deviations. With Figure 65, the CEOs salary is over 3 <u>feet</u> away from the average.

We considered the case for all data in Figure 7 with its resulting 37 standard deviations and 3 feet distance to reach $1,000,000, let us now consider the more realistic case of Figure 66. Using the revised values of $33,580 as an average and standard deviation of $11,986, the compensation gap overruns the ruler to ($1,000,000 - $33,580) / $11,986 = 80.6 inches (rounded), or more than 6 feet 8 inches to reach the hypothetical CEO's salary, much more if reality indicates salaries are larger for executives.

Another factor worthy of evaluation is the change in standard deviation values. Standard deviation for Figure 65 is $25,827 and Figure 66 is $11,986. Using Figure 66's data results in over a 53% reduction in wage variability that is directly attributable to a large range of compensation values in the right tail of this distribution: (1 - ($11,986 / $25,827)) * 100 = 53.6% (rounded).

7 COMPENSATION AND BONUS METRICS

The previous sections addressing corporate history, basic statistical properties, and numerous figures representing data within 30 industries have brought us to this point. Analyses of these industries result from data within the United States, but possesses international connections to economic performance of publicly traded corporations. Previous investigation and papers by researchers provide links to national wage distributions connecting many countries worldwide and the analysis within this text demonstrates a link to these studies at a national, industry level. Stock exchanges in many countries list publicly traded corporations for countries around the world. The establishment of ties to industry distributions in this book with links to national distributions provides a means to reduce excessive compensation and improve economic performance of corporations globally.

Leading up to this section is a preponderance of data demonstrating that salaries of CEOs and other senior executives are excessive. It is difficult to dismiss arguments that these salaries are not excessive when considering the upper 20% of industry distributions possess more range than the lower 80% of a workforce as well as creating a large percentage of the overall statistical deviation. Upon removing the upper 20% of data, the lower 80% takes on properties associated with a normal distribution. When one considers a hypothetical maximum CEO salary limitation of only $1,000,000 and scaling standard deviations to one inch each, the number of standard deviations required from the mean, as presented in Figure 6, to attain this level of income results in distances measured in feet, not inches. If someone possessed talent as rare as 1/1,000,000 individuals, the standard deviations extending outward from the average would not exceed 4.75 inches. Attempting to justify maximum salaries with a limitation of only a hypothetical $1,000,000, not considering those who receive much more, seems ludicrous as the observed number of standard deviations involved would create such a rarity of individuals that they would theoretically exceed the number of people who have lived on the planet in all of history. This hypothetical $1,000,000 limitation and analyses does not take into consideration the multi-million dollar bonuses frequently reported in the media.

The numerous figures presented prior to this chapter clearly show a majority of workforce personnel within these industries receive compensation at a level determined by the normal statistical distribution while managers and executives receive compensation by another scheme. Both groups are company employees. Social responsibility for fair treatment of workers as well as the fairness principle (ethical principle involving justice) requires all employees to compensation in a similar manner.

Characteristics previously discussed and compared involve individuals in executive positions, upper management, and personnel in the rank-and-file workforce. Previous research by numerous individuals into analysis of unique executive qualities has failed to define special characteristics or abilities that set these individuals apart from other company employees. The ethical sense of justice and attention in recent years to corporate social responsibility requires meeting ethical responsibilities. Typically, the principles of fairness include rewarding individuals according to their efforts that contribute to results, the merits that individuals and groups possess, and other relevant properties such as education and experience.

People within organizations need to feel a company respects and values their efforts and contributions. People do not like the impression of injustice in compensation and reward systems – that they are merely a means to achieve a result. People's personal interactions communicate feelings of injustice seen or experienced throughout the corporate hierarchy and this spread of distrust or feelings of unfair actions can permeate all organizational levels.

Corporate cultures that focus on the individual recognize a need for a range of exchanges to take place between employees and the company. People within an organization come to expect compensation based on the equity model – one that recognizes contributions made by an organization's individuals toward goal achievement. In light of previously presented industry analyses, there is great difficulty understanding any level of equity principle application when a huge number of standard deviations exist between the industry average wage and a theoretical $1,000,000 CEO salary and reality shows this to be much more. Logic dictates that no single individual can be this much more productive or valuable than the industry average and research indicates this productivity level to be much less.

There is no reason or logic in providing management compensation in the millions of dollars with bonuses in the multiples of base salaries when data clearly shows this a preferential treatment when compared to a large majority of employees. The lack of research data correlating additional effort and contribution of CEOs to overall corporate outcomes further indicates this is a situation where those in a position to loot the corporate piggy bank are doing so at shareholder expense. The practices of rewarding departing executives beyond contract requirements is a violation of those contracts – as well as well ignoring ethical principles because ethical limits do not exist when these practices exceed contractual obligations. Has anyone noticed how lawsuits are filed when contract obligations are violated, but not when someone receives more reward than was bargained?

Additionally, one should consider a comparison of ethical actions at opposite ends of compensation scales. In recent years, there exist numerous examples of unethical practices where corporations pay barely existence level wages through subsidiary companies in other countries to employ children and other workers in order to make products at prices that are more competitive and / or to reap additional profit. Human rights and other groups bring these practices to light and force a change in practice due to public outrage. There appears a thread of logic in assuming that if it is not ethical to pay existence level wages in order to increase a corporation's advantage in a market, then at the other end of this scale it is also not ethical to pay excessive wages to executives and thereby decrease a corporation's economic competiveness through wasteful expenditure of resources.

Developing a Metric

A good metric has several characteristics associated with it, among them a quantitative element so it is easy to use numbers associated with the element. Creating a foundation for a good metric also requires an easy understanding of terminology and methods by those using them to improve reaching a defined goal. When deciding upon and deploying a metric, the information gathered must be useful in aligning strategic and tactical goals and methods.

Metrics, in a simple sense, are standards comparing achievements against a minimum or maximum limitation or requirement. The setting of executive salaries is an internal process within a corporation that can be influenced by external actions of judicial and regulatory bodies. More and more in recent years there is a perception factor connecting corporate and other stakeholders to results linking social responsibility, public outrage, and ethics when considering executive compensation levels. One element of a good metric is an ability to create process improvement. A second characteristic is that a metric is specific in targeting what needs measurement. Third, there is an ability to obtain complete and accurate data. Metrics also allow flexibility in gathering data at the time when needed. Metrics that maintain simplicity in their approach do not require detailed explanation to create an understanding of what they do and therefore are easier to promote to the constituency; whether it is to corporate rank-and-file employees, congress, investors, or judiciary bodies. Simplicity also creates a stronger effect on people and processes because of ease in internalizing their value.

Several traits are associated with poor metrics and are opposite those described above. First, the methodology does not allow collecting accurate and/or complete data. Another poor characteristic is creating a standard that allows people to game the system or in other words just make numbers, as this is not in the best interests of establishing a standard – regardless of the element under evaluation. Standards that are easily changed and manipulated make poor metrics and the same goes for creating a large number of metrics because they result in increased overhead cost and administration becomes very cumbersome. Complex metrics create difficulty both in understanding how they function and in execution.

Therefore, these factors result in construction of metrics that fail to achieve their intended purpose and / or create great frustration in trying to measure and achieve goals.

Paying CEOs What They Are Worth

One of the statements made at the beginning of this book is that CEOs would not be happy when paid what they are worth. The information presented for individuals in thirty industries makes it possible to derive a quantitative metric based on the normal distribution when addressing a corporate workforce. Each industry's income clearly demonstrates that at least 80% of a workforce follows a normal statistical distribution. Properties of a normal statistical distribution allow determining a central tendency of data (mean or average) and a standard deviation describing the rate of variation within a data set. These properties allow calculating where a person is located in this distribution.

A method that determines what an individual is worth within a corporation is a simple one to employ. Let us consider as an example, a company with 6285 employees and a corporate structure with managers, executives, vice-presidents, presidents, and CEO. The CEO is the top-ranked individual with a corporate position of 1/6285 or 0.000159 and as such, logic indicates he or she should be the highest paid in a normal distribution. We will also use an average of $51,900 and standard deviation of $25,000 for the 80% majority of industry income in calculating what a CEO's compensation should be, since CEOs are also company employees.

There is a normal statistical distribution chart to seven decimal points in the appendix. To move from the mean to one standard deviation is equal to 50% (all values left of the mean) plus additional movement to the right. If we move one standard deviation to the right, we cover 0.5000000 + 0.3413447 = 0.8413447 or 84.13% of a workforce. If we consider only our hypothetical CEO's ordinal position described above, he or she falls into the chart at 1 − 0.000159 or 0.999841 or approximately 3.6 standard deviations. This makes his or her base pay a maximum of $51,900 + (3.6 x $25,000) = $141,900, the cutoff defining a limit for normal compensation based on workforce data and above which excessive compensation begins when paying a CEO what they are worth.

The question now before us: Does this methodology make a good metric? Using the above criteria, we have the following.

Are numerical terms easily associated with the element in question?

Is there an easy understanding of the methods and terminology?

Does this method provide a useful way to achieve strategic and tactical goals?

Does this method define a limitation or threshold?

Does this method provide a specific target for the measured element?

Does this method provide for collection of complete and accurate data?

Does this method allow timely data collection?

Does the method prevent individuals from manipulation of the outcomes?

The answer to all these questions is yes. The number of employees within a corporation is easily determined by examining the number of employees on a payroll, a number that human resources or finance can provide. This method and terminology follow simple mathematics and examination of a normal statistical distribution table. Some of a corporation's strategic and tactical goals usually involve creating competition in a market to attain increased market share and to become more competitive against direct competitors. There is the possibility of directing resources from reduced overhead toward product improvement or increased research and development for new market offerings. This method provides meeting the requirement of a limitation and there is a specific target. Collection of complete and accurate data is possible with execution in a timely manner. Attempts to manipulate corporate data for employee annual income and number of employees would not be easy because these are factors having oversight of numerous individuals as well as reporting requirements to federal and state governments. Next I will present an alternate method to the one described above and it provides greater income for CEOs.

The Bounds' Executive Compensation Metrics

One of the problems with executive salaries and bonuses is

no apparent limit or reason to salaries and bonus amounts. The Bounds' Executive Compensation Metrics provide two data based methods for determining where excessive executive compensation starts for CEOs. One method utilizes industry-based data and the other corporate-based data. Definition of these metrics originated in: *Wage Distributions and Defining a Metric for Excessive Compensation.*[1]

Let us now consider another comment made at the beginning of this book, that executives would not be happy even though they were paid as though they were as rare as one in a million individuals. Reference the normal statistical distribution chart in the appendix. Using our CEO example from before let us make our CEO a rare individual, one that has a truly special trait for this position (though none ever defined) that surfaces only one in a million or 0.000001 individuals. The Bounds' Executive Compensation Threshold - Industry and Bounds' Executive Compensation Threshold – Corporation metrics are easy to calculate and use the normal distribution as a foundation that defines a limit on normal compensation and where excessive executive compensation begins based on the lower 80% of an industry's or corporation's income:

$$\bar{X}_i + 4.75\sigma_i \qquad (1)$$

or

$$\bar{X}_c + 4.75\sigma_c , \qquad (2)$$

where $\bar{X}_i$ and $\bar{X}_c$ represent the average income of the lower 80% of an industry's or corporation's income and $4.75\sigma_i$ and $4.75\sigma_c$ represent the number of standard deviations to reach 1/1,000,000 multiplied by the standard deviation for an industry or corporation.

We will again use our example based on hypothetical data with an industry's income average of $51,900 (high for most companies in this book) for the lower 80% of a workforce and a standard deviation of $25,000. Moving right from the average to 4.75 standard deviations on the normal distribution table makes a person one in one-million or $(1 - (.9999990))*1,000,000 = 1$. This allows a CEO to be paid as though they are one in a million and makes his or her normal pay a maximum of $51,900 + (4.75 * $25,000) = $170,650, above which excessive compensation begins within this hypothetical industry. Depending upon a company's position within an industry and pay structure, a company's board of directors could set maximum compensation lower without violating this data based metric. However, compensation beyond this value is excessive when using industry-based data. The corporation definition in equation (2) is an alternative when a board of directors elects this option based on company data that that they feel is significant from its operating industry.

The question now before us: Do these methodologies make a good metric? Using the previous criteria for constructing a good metric, the answer is yes. Determining a number of employees within an industry or corporation is easy by examining reports issued annually by the federal government or corporate finances. Because industry data is not likely to change rapidly over a short time period, calculation of this factor could be annually if chosen by a board or for a time interval of years at which time rates are subject to revision. Standard annual pay increases would apply based on equitable levels received by the overall industry or corporate workforce. This method and terminology follow simple mathematical calculations using a normal statistical distribution table, provides for meeting the requirement of a limitation, and there is a specific target. Some of a corporation's strategic and tactical goals usually involve creating competition in a market to attain increased market share and become more competitive against direct competitors. There is the possibility of directing resources from reduced overhead toward product improvement or increased research and development for new market offerings. This method provides for meeting the requirements of a limitation and a specific target. Collection of complete and accurate data is possible with execution in a timely manner. Attempts to manipulate industry or corporate data and standard deviation would not be easy because these are factors having oversight of numerous individuals as well as federal and state government reporting.

The logic behind The Bounds' Executive Compensation Thresholds is simple. First, no publicly traded company within the United States or any other country has 1,000,000 or more employees. Therefore, using a 1,000,000-person standard is very generous. Second, the United States census for 2010 was slightly under 309 million – indicating that if a CEO were to possess a trait needed for their position that was truly this rare, theoretically, there could only be a maximum of 309 within the population, but there is no such trait or skill definition. There are many more CEOs of companies within the United States than 309 within the Fortune 500 companies alone and many thousands of senior managers and other executive positions exist below the CEO and above the 80% wage distributions defining the majority of industry or corporate workforces.

The Bounds Bonus Metric

Many people on corporate payrolls may not receive a bonus for their yearly contributions to corporate outcomes. Hiring was at a given rate of pay, hourly or salary, and upon reaching the end of the year they receive their last paycheck for that accounting period and file income taxes. If for some reason there is employment termination during the year, vacation time and so forth is included in their last compensation check, and severance may or may not be included due to company policy and circumstances. Generally, the attitude is one of discarding an employee because of compensation ending according to a hiring agreement, no above and beyond awards of corporate monetary resources, and no special offers of consulting or additional involvement with the corporation as many times announced when CEOs and other executives "seek other employment opportunities."

There appears no limit to the vast sums of corporate resources showered on executives in the form of bonuses. Next, we will consider metrics based on industry or corporate data for bonuses paid to executives. A board of directors may wish to allocate bonuses at a rate less than described below, however, the Bounds' Bonus Metric is the maximum for this compensation metric and amounts exceeding this limit are excessive by definition:

Bounds' Bonus Metric = Maximum of 1 Standard Deviation of the Lower 80% of Company or Industry Workforce Income, dependent on using either the industry or company method to calculate the excessive compensation value as stated in equations (1) or (2) respectively.

A board of directors would perform the calculation when selecting an industry or corporate option using the latest available data. With all 30 industries studied, one standard deviation represents a range of values when compared to average workforce income. These percentages represent a significant amount of income for a majority of people working within these industries and the companies they represent, much more so than the cost of living increase these individuals are likely to receive in annual wage and salary increases. Therefore, using a data derived metric based on an industry's or corporate's standard deviation is more than generous when aligning executive and management compensation. Using the principle of employing ethical limits, a single standard deviation based cap on bonuses founded on an industry's or corporation's workforce establishes relevance to this group in defining a quantitative limit.

Using our previous question to evaluate this metric: Do these methodologies make a good metric? Reviewing our previous requirements on what constitutes good metrics results in one answer to all these questions, yes. Numerical data is easily associated with the element, methods and terminology are easy to understand, strategic and tactical goal achievement is possible, there is a definition of a limit and a specific target; complete, accurate, and timely data collection is possible; and this method prevents easy data manipulation to achieve a desired outcome.

Using our previous example of paying a CEO what he or she is worth, if this company achieved a good business year, a CEO's maximum income would be $141,900 + $25,000 = 166,900 when adding in a maximum of one standard deviation as defined by the Bounds' Bonus Metric. Of course, a company's board of directors could set maximum compensation lower and reduce the bonus due to business conditions.

Recent history records many incidents of public outcry at excessive compensation amounts in salaries and bonuses in various media. The situation was one of viewpoint, opinion, point and counterpoint, which left all parties involved at the point where they started – without resolution and no methodology to define in quantitative terms what constitutes excessive executive compensation metrics for salary and bonuses. This was the situation until research provided metrics for excessive compensation levels. These metrics create ethical and easily verifiable limitations for compensation.

There is no logical reason to reward any employee with a bonus in the millions of dollars when 80% of the workforce's average yearly income is much lower as illustrated in the industry analysis figures presented in graphic detail earlier in this book. The bonus metric for individuals falling outside the lower 80% of a company or industry's employees is a simple definition based on quantitative data.

Should boards of directors, courts, and legislative actions implement these data driven metrics defining excessive compensation and bonuses based on similar analysis as illustrated for these 30 industries, there is no doubt these actions will leave executives screaming from the rooftops. There will without doubt be accusations and challenges, false statements, and innuendos foretelling the imminent demise of corporate performance in application of these compensation metrics for executive pay. I do not believe they are valid and their crystal balls not shiny enough to make such predictions.

Some people may think these limitations will prohibit attracting the best and brightest management talent, but this is not true. Where will the talent go when an overall application of these metrics create a standard defining an excessive compensation threshold for salaries and bonuses? One argument is that talented individuals will go into better paying fields. The most likely move will be to attain positions within industries that pay higher overall salaries, but this only increases the competition and selection within a larger talent pool and creates an overflow of talent into companies of other industries. If we use our previous CEO example, the truth is many people in the current workforce will aspire to a salary of almost $141,900 (more with bonus possibilities). It is doubtful there will be a shortage of talented applicants. One must also consider the roll down effect.

Until this point, there has not been a discussion of the roll down effect. What happens when there is alignment of CEO salaries using the excessive compensation metrics described in this book? The short story is that these effects are huge. CEOs will not settle for salaries lesser than their subordinates on the organizational chart. Salaries of lesser-ranked corporate executives are going to drop as senior alignment occurs to these metrics. There are many types of organizations, but consider an organizational structure that has a CEO, and Vice-Presidents of Operations, Sales and Marketing, Human Resources, Environmental Health and Safety, General Council, Corporate Quality, and Global Ethics and Compliance. Let us set a current CEO's basic salary at $1,000,000 and the vice presidents' at $500,000. Dropping the CEO's salary to $141,900 may drop salaries in the next tier to $100,000 or less. This is an immediate savings of $858,100 + (7 x 400,000) = $3,658,000 and this does not take into account limited bonus rewards and further roll down to lesser executives and managers – remember these people are overhead and this is just one hypothetical company within an industry. With some companies having a CEO salary in the millions, the roll down effect creates huge corporate savings that can easily reach tens of millions of dollars per year – much larger savings across industries. Corporate boards need to consider the fact that current compensation methods are far out of line with social responsibility requirements, do not follow ethical practices, and restrict competitive practices within modern organizations because they are too expensive to continue.

Theory of Executive Compensation Saturation

Up to this point the analyses has been directed toward a single industry or application to a publicly traded corporation having only one entity, but what about corporations possessing oversight of multiple companies that may represent more than one industry? Multiple industry / niche corporations require consideration in addressing additional responsibilities in this broader context while realizing, whether admitting to it or not, everyone has a limited effective span of control – there is no all-seeing or all-knowing among human beings.

Anyone having undertaken a task involving people understands there is a limit to how many people one person can effectively provide oversight. There is a limit to effective team size in accomplishing any goal. The ability to broaden a CEOs span of control becomes more constrained when considering operations in multiple countries, each having their own idiosyncrasies for business operations, and further restrictions due to different operating times when changing time zones. Increased complexity requires additional delegation of authority to maintain effectiveness and results in less and less direct CEO oversight. Operations in multiple industries also restricts the amount of detailed knowledge one person can possess concerning each one's overall requirements and functions, which requires out of necessity that any knowledge possessed be more general in nature. These factors increase the value of arguments against how much CEOs contribute to wealth creation in a publicly traded corporation. Known and taught for many years in management courses, the money factor decreases in its ability to keep individuals motivated after meeting basic needs, in short, a point of diminishing returns. Other factors must take over and drive an individual to accomplishment and realization of individual worth.

I ranked previous theories of executive management compensation into the category of myth early on in this book. They provided little insight into data driven outcomes and only offered guidance in the most general of terms without a means to determine if they were valid. I would be remiss in dismissing previous theories without offering one for replacement. The Theory of Executive Compensation Saturation addresses a CEO's value to organizational operations and after reaching this limit saturation occurs and there is no further value to corporate realization. For calculating executive compensation, the equations result in:

$$\bar{X}_i + 4.75\sigma_i + B_{i1} + .9B_{i2} + .8B_{i3} + \ldots + .1B_{i10}, \qquad (3)$$

or

$$\bar{X}_c + 4.75\sigma_c + B_{c1} + .9B_{c2} + .8B_{c3} + \ldots + .1B_{c10}, \qquad (4)$$

where $\bar{X}_i$ and $\bar{X}_c$ represent either the lower 80% of industry average or lower 80% of corporation average income respectively
and,
σ_i and σ_c represent either the lower 80% of industry or lower 80% of corporate standard deviation
and,
B_{i1} and B_{c1} represent the potential single based on one industry or one corporate standard deviation, using the lower 80% of industry or corporate income. Corporations possessing oversight of multiple companies within an industry or a possibility of multiple industries extends the bonus factor to include $.9B_{i2}$ to $.1B_{i10}$ or $.9B_{c2}$ to $.1B_{c10}$ in order of largest to smallest $\bar{X}_i$ or $\bar{X}_c$ because the standard deviation determines data spread about the mean and not vice versa. The additional bonuses in these equations drive additional motivation of an executive to manage a broader range of interests while recognizing the limits of a span of control. The maximum number of companies or industries included in the bonus calculation is limited

to ten as shown, after which there is no additional compensation.

Addition of one standard deviation for a bonus effectively brings compensation levels to a theoretical threshold of $\overline{X}_i + 5.75\sigma_i$, which is equal to 4 in one billion individuals. Realization of the bonus amounts is not during the year, but awarded at year's end according to policy. If awarded quarterly, total award reduces to a calculated 1/4 of maximum or less as determined by the board of directors. With the world's population slightly over 7 billion in 2010, year of the industry data displayed in this text, there should be no more than approximately 28 individuals on the planet, should a truly rare executive talent exist, and therefore, a generous rate of remuneration.

Reasoning for de-rating additional bonuses due to multiple company / industry involvement in large corporations is simple. Additional companies place increased loads on an executive for oversight, each having unique situations requiring his or her involvement to varying degrees, but they are not equal and executive loading shifts as situations change. A company composed of 5 entities placing a load on an executive for performance issues of 30%, 20%, 15%, 25%, and 10% maximize available time without reaching the maximum number of 10 industries / companies. If there are more than this, it is not possible for an executive to provide adequate oversight and something must go aside and therefore, the limit of 10 bonus elements comprising additional compensation.

The Theory of Executive Compensation Saturation quantitatively defines compensation for executives with increased span of control responsibilities while recognizing the limitations of individuals. Saturation limits imposed by de-rating factors curtail excessive compensation. As an example, we will consider a company that has the largest average income with nine additional corporations, each in separate industries. Using equation (3) and substituting data we have a hypothetical situation:

$53,388 + 4.75(21,538) + 21,538 + .9(24,172) + .8(17,235) + .7(18,222) + .6(14,002) + .5(16,232) + .4(15,177) + .3(17,650) + .2(13,886) + .1(17,289) = $257,919$ or 4.8 (rounded) times the average salary.

This results in a pay level (after subtracting the industry average) that is approximately 9.5 standard deviations above the average, far above the planet's population in probability of occurrence.

Even a casual browsing of the Occupation Listing in the appendices is impressive when one considers the numerous elements needed to create and make a company or industry function. Consider the backgrounds of people working within a company. Individuals dedicate years to building a career through practicing the varied and related aspects of an occupation. Each of these is unique because the individuals have different experiences and relate to technical and general topics in different ways. Their background experiences forms different paths of thinking that have a range of viewpoints that contribute diverse inputs to problem definitions and solution determination on and off the job. Life experiences whether male or female, athlete, scholar, artist, rich, poor, or middle class and so forth contribute in ways that populate a workforce at all levels with tremendous diversity for creativity and achievement.

Skill levels result from dedication to a broad range of activities. No one skill is simply doing one thing, but draws upon experience, training, education, and many other traits of an individual. Some people approach an occupation from a creative and artistic viewpoint, others from a viewpoint of service to people and their fellow man, while still others are more technically inclined and relate to mechanical or theoretical functions of equipment and the world. Other skills relate to physical activities involved with sports, outdoor industries, and so on. The skills required in a company or industry is broad in range, diverse in application, and makes these areas of consideration complex with much variation from one individual to another.

Education is a multifaceted area within the occupational theater. As levels of knowledge grow, so do the areas of specialization. This results from a need to understand more complex and diverse areas within a body of knowledge. These factors are easy to understand when considering the many different fields of engineering, medicine, research, education, and technical applications of electronics, construction, equipment maintenance, and many other trade occupations. Gone are the days when a person could learn all they need to know from a father, mother, uncle, or aunt. These areas consistently require higher levels of education and refresher courses to stay abreast of current requirements and to maintain professional credentials and licenses.

No one person could ever hope to attain such broad levels of expertise and knowledge to honestly say they alone created the wealth realized on a company's balance sheet, but this is one of the justifications frequently put forth in justifying huge salaries and staggering amounts paid in bonuses to some individuals as a reward for corporate performance. This must be the height of hubris if anyone truly believes their actions alone result in achieving this impossible goal. One thing I have learned in my professional and educational journey is the more I learn, the more I understand there is a vast amount of things that I do not understand and will not ever be able to comprehend if for no other reason than the mind has limitations and one's lifespan is finite.

The preponderance of data presented in graphic detail supports the conclusion that chief executive officers of publicly traded companies and many other lesser ranking corporate officials are excessively compensated. As with other company employees, they require compensation for their contribution to a company's overall performance, but to a much lesser degree than currently in practice and it should be much more in line with the majority of an industry's or corporation's workforce. The CEO in many cases deserve compensation at a level below the one-in-a-million metric limitation and ethical and social responsibility actions toward implementing these metrics can result in saving millions of dollars to companies by reducing overhead. Bonuses should also be much more in line with industry or corporate data, in this case the Bounds' Bonus Metric, as previously defined. Even at a standard deviation level for a bonus, this amount represents significant recognition when compared to what an individual in an industry or corporate workforce would receive. These metrics have enormous national and international economic implications when applying the savings toward continuous product improvement, development of new products and services, and returning value to shareholders while providing additional job growth and making corporations more competitive within a global economy.

8 EPILOG

The basic problem in beginning research and writing for this book was how to overcome the general, nonspecific term "excessive" as it applies to executive compensation levels. Excessive is a very nebulous term subject to a wide variety of meanings and interpretations of quantity that are dependent upon individual viewpoints. Excessive noise levels are defined in decibels, dB, too much rain at one time in relation to flood stages, but excessive compensation in relation to what? This question raises awareness of a need for qualifying the term. How can you pay someone too much? Too much would seem to relate somehow to the majority of a workforce. Whatever the result, an obvious element in the solution would be an ability to relate this term to economic income levels. Therefore, the problem definition became one of how to define "excessive" executive compensation in a way that allows practical application to the process of establishing an executive compensation upper limit metric.

To measure excessive compensation requires a non-arbitrary method and by its nature, income units of measurement. In this application measurement uses monetary units in U. S. dollars representing yearly income for the year 2010. Addressing yearly income of personnel employed in the various industries created links to both employees and national business economic levels of income. Because a CEO and other managers are company employees, relevancy is established to results of industry income levels.

Analysis indicated income for industry groups were related to national level income studies, applicable to normal statistical distributions, and these factors provided a means for evaluation. Statistical results in some cases demonstrated links to lognormal distributions at a national level and in all cases the normal distribution at industry levels. End results demonstrate a link to international economic studies, national economic results, and individual economic sectors of industry.

Correlation to national and international economic studies and established statistical processes allowed creation of specific data-based metrics based on a mathematical model for industry groups that also possesses the flexibility of application to individual companies. The metric relates to the element under evaluation, establishes a limit, and is not ambiguous. Use of this metric removes the stigma of excessive executive compensation and makes the process of establishing compensation more transparent for all stakeholders. The bonus metric also possesses these properties while curtailing lavish and highly questionable rewards focused on a single individual or small group of individuals that overlook the contributions of the majority of a company's workforce. Additional flexibility is also provided in the bonus metric for companies involved in multiple industry and niche operations.

Application of these metrics, enforcement, and control through stakeholders, legislative actions, regulatory bodies, and judicial actions will result in curtailing excessive compensation. Groups involved in oversight of ethical performance, social responsibility ratings, and corporate governance actions can exercise influence to require adherence to these metrics. How well this information is used and enforced now falls on implementation by these individuals and groups. Current methods of executive compensation are far too costly to continue and cannot be rationally justified. The challenge in now in the hands of the public and responsible organizations to take this information and implement action for change and compensation control.

9 CHAPTER REFERENCES

Chapter 2

[1, 3] Kaufman, J. (2008). Corporate law and the sovereignty of states. *American Sociological Review, 73*(3), 402-425.

[2] Smith, A. (1776). The wealth of nations. New York, New York: Bantam Dell

[4] Brown, J. R. (2008). Returning fairness to executive compensation. *North Dakota Law Review, 84*(4), 1141-1159.

[5] Dobson, J. (1993). The role of ethics in finance. *Financial Analysts Journal, 49*(6), 57-61.

[6, 7, 10] Corley, R., Shedd, P., & Holmes, E. (1986). *Principles of business law* (13th ed.). Englewood Cliffs, NJ: Prentice-Hall.

[8, 11] Hill, C. A., & McDonnell, B. H. (2007). Disney, good faith, and structural bias. *Journal of Corporation Law, 32*(4), 833-864.

[9] Forbes, D. P., & Milliken, F. J. (1999). Cognition and corporate governance: Understanding boards of directors as strategic decision-making groups. *Academy of Management Review, 24*(3), 489-505.

[12, 21] Grant, G. H. (2003). The evolution of corporate governance and its impact on modern corporate America. *Management Decision, 41*(9), 923-934.

[13] Atkinson, A., & Salterios, S. (2002). Taking control of the corporate governance quandary. *CMA Management, 76*(6), 23-27

[14] Coakley, J., & Iliopoulou, S. (2006). Bidder CEO and other executive compensation in UK M&As. *European Financial Management, 12*(4), 609-631. doi: 10.1111/j.1468-036X.2006.00333.x.

[15, 19] Bebchuk, L. A., & Fried, J. M. (2004). Pay without performance: Overview of the issues. *Journal of Corporation Law, 30*(4), 647-673.

[16] Barlas, S. (2008). Corporate pay. *Financial Executive, 24*(3), 26-29

[17] Bounds, J. L. (2012). Wage distributions and defining a metric for excessive compensation. Doctoral dissertation, Argosy University, Phoenix, Arizona.

[18] Panitz, P. G. (2009). Executive compensation: What's reasonable? *Journal of Accountancy, 207*(6), 56-61.

[20] Chaudhri, V. (2003). Executive compensation: Understanding the issues. *Australian Economic Review, 36*(3), 300-305. doi: 10.1111/1467-8462.00289

[22, 25] Conyon, M. J. (2011). Executive compensation consultants and CEO pay. *Vanderbilt Law Review, 64*(2), 397-428.

[23] Kolev, G. I. (2008). The stock market bubble, shareholders' attribution bias and excessive top CEO pay. *Journal of Behavioral Finance, 9*(2), 62-71. doi: 10.1080/15427560802093647

[24] Gordon, J. N. (2005). Executive compensation: If there's a problem, what's the remedy? The case for "compensation discussion and analysis." *Journal of Corporation Law, 30*(4), 675-702.

[26] Anabtawi, I. (2005). Explaining pay without performance: The tournament alternative. *Emory Law Journal, 54*(4), 1557-1602.

[27] Groysberg, B., McLean, A. N., & Nohria, N. (2006). Are leaders portable? *Harvard Business Review, 84*(5), 92-100.

[28] Drennan, W. A. (2008). The pirates will party on! The nonqualified deferred compensation rules will not prevent CEOs from acting like plundering pirates and should be scuttled. *Vermont Law Review, 33*(1), 1-41.

[29] Woolard, E. (2006). CEOs are being paid too much. *Across the Board, 43*(1), 28-30.

[30] Chan, M. (2008). Executive compensation. *Business & Society Review, 113*(1), 129-161.doi: 10.1111/j.1467-8594.2008.00316.x

[31] Grubb, D. (1985). Ability and power over production in the distribution of earnings. *Review of Economics & Statistics, 67*(2), 188-194.

Chapter 3

United States Department of Labor (2011). Bureau of Labor Statistics, occupational employment statistics, May 2010 occupational employment and wage estimates, national sector NAICS industry-specific estimates.

Chapter 4

[1] Chatterjee, A., Sinha, S., & Chakrabarti, B. K. (2007). Economic inequality: Is it natural? *Current* Science, 92(10), 1383-1389.

[2] Nirei, M., & Souma, W. (2007). A two factor model of income distribution dynamics. *Review of Income and Wealth, 53*(3), 440-459.

[3] Lubrano, M. (2011). The econometrics of inequality and poverty. Lecture 4: Lorenz curves, the Gini coefficient and parametric distributions.

[4] Champernowne, D. G. (1952). The graduation of income distributions. *Econometrics, 20*(4).

[5] Grubb, D. (1985). Ability and power over production in the distribution of earnings. *Review of Economics & Statistics, 67*(2), 188-194.

[6] Chatterjee, A., Sinha, S., & Chakrabarti, B. K. (2007). Economic inequality: Is it natural? *Current* Science, 92(10), 1383-1389.

[7] Jagielski, M., & Kutner, R. (2010). Study of households' income in Poland by using the statistical physics approach. *Acta Physica Polonica A., 117*(4), 615-618.

[8] Montroll, E. W., & Shlesinger, M. F. (1982). On 1/f noise and other distributions with long tails. *Proceedings of the National Academy of Science, 79*, 3380-3382.

Chapter 7

[1] Bounds, J. L. (2012). Wage distributions and defining a metric for excessive compensation. Doctoral dissertation, Argosy University, Phoenix, Arizona.

APPENDIX A

NORMAL DISTRIBUTION

The normal distribution table. This table starts at the average (mean) shown as 0.0 in the left column and continues to the right using 0.00 in the top, left row with a value of 0.5000000. Where these two intersect indicates how much of the normal distribution is to the left of this point. Seven decimal places provide for readings to ten-millionths. Use the following steps to determine what you need to know concerning a location on the normal distribution.

1. Find a specific standard deviation value by using the left column first and then the last digit using the top row or alternatively find a value you are interested in and the left column and top row will indicate the standard deviation value. The values in the table indicate the percentage of the normal distribution covered to that point.

2. Use the following method to determine how many units per million are covered at a particular standard deviation value:

(1 – value from table) x 1,000,000 = number of units

For example, at the intersection of 4.7 left column and 0.05 (4.75) top column is 0.9999990 and to find the units per million: (1 – 0.9999990) x 1,000,000 = 1. If we were looking to pay a CEO in an industry as though he or she was as rare as one-in-a-million, he or she would have a pay standard deviation of the mean industry value plus 4.75 times the industry standard deviation. If we were looking to pay the CEO using the mean company value (using an 80% cutoff for data) and company normal distribution value, substitute these, but the calculation is then the same

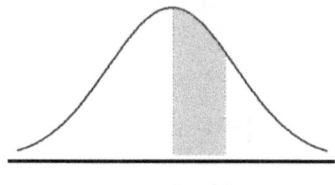

0 and Z

Area Between 0 and Z

Normal Distribution Table Starting at Mean of 0 to Z

Z	0.00	0.01	0.02	0.03	0.04
0.0	0.0000000	0.0039894	0.0079783	0.0119665	0.0159534
0.1	0.0398278	0.0437953	0.0477584	0.0517168	0.0556700
0.2	0.0792597	0.0831662	0.0870644	0.0909541	0.0948349
0.3	0.1179114	0.1217195	0.1255158	0.1293000	0.1330717
0.4	0.1554217	0.1590970	0.1627573	0.1664022	0.1700314
0.5	0.1914625	0.1949743	0.1984682	0.2019440	0.2054015
0.6	0.2257469	0.2290691	0.2323711	0.2356527	0.2389137
0.7	0.2580363	0.2611479	0.2642375	0.2673049	0.2703500
0.8	0.2881446	0.2910299	0.2938919	0.2967306	0.2995458
0.9	0.3159399	0.3185887	0.3212136	0.3238145	0.3263912
1.0	0.3413447	0.3437524	0.3461358	0.3484950	0.3508300
1.1	0.3643339	0.3665005	0.3686431	0.3707619	0.3728568
1.2	0.3849303	0.3868606	0.3887676	0.3906514	0.3925123
1.3	0.4031995	0.4049021	0.4065825	0.4082409	0.4098773
1.4	0.4192433	0.4207302	0.4221962	0.4236415	0.4250663
1.5	0.4331928	0.4344783	0.4357445	0.4369916	0.4382198
1.6	0.4452007	0.4463011	0.4473839	0.4484493	0.4494974
1.7	0.4554345	0.4563671	0.4572838	0.4581849	0.4590705
1.8	0.4640697	0.4648521	0.4656205	0.4663750	0.4671159
1.9	0.4712834	0.4719334	0.4725711	0.4731966	0.4738102
2.0	0.4772499	0.4777844	0.4783083	0.4788217	0.4793248
2.1	0.4821356	0.4825708	0.4829970	0.4834142	0.4838226
2.2	0.4860966	0.4864474	0.4867906	0.4871263	0.4874545
2.3	0.4892759	0.4895559	0.4898296	0.4900969	0.4903581

0.05	0.06	0.07	0.08	0.09
0.0199388	0.0239222	0.0279032	0.0318814	0.0358564
0.0596177	0.0635595	0.0674949	0.0714237	0.0753454
0.0987063	0.1025681	0.1064199	0.1102612	0.1140919
0.1368307	0.1405764	0.1443088	0.1480273	0.1517317
0.1736448	0.1772419	0.1808225	0.1843863	0.1879331
0.2088403	0.2122603	0.2156612	0.2190427	0.2224047
0.2421539	0.2453731	0.2485711	0.2517478	0.2549029
0.2733726	0.2763727	0.2793501	0.2823046	0.2852361
0.3023375	0.3051055	0.3078498	0.3105703	0.3132671
0.3289439	0.3314724	0.3339768	0.3364569	0.3389129
0.3531409	0.3554277	0.3576903	0.3599289	0.3621434
0.3749281	0.3769756	0.3789995	0.3809999	0.3829768
0.3943502	0.3961653	0.3979577	0.3997274	0.4014747
0.4114920	0.4130850	0.4146565	0.4162067	0.4177356
0.4264707	0.4278550	0.4292191	0.4305634	0.4318879
0.4394292	0.4406201	0.4417924	0.4429466	0.4440826
0.4505285	0.4515428	0.4525403	0.4535213	0.4544860
0.4599408	0.4607961	0.4616364	0.4624620	0.4632730
0.4678432	0.4685572	0.4692581	0.4699460	0.4706210
0.4744119	0.4750021	0.4755808	0.4761482	0.4767045
0.4798178	0.4803007	0.4807738	0.4812372	0.4816911
0.4842224	0.4846137	0.4849966	0.4853713	0.4857379
0.4877755	0.4880894	0.4883962	0.4886962	0.4889893
0.4906133	0.4908625	0.4911060	0.4913437	0.4915758

Z	0.00	0.01	0.02	0.03	0.04
2.4	0.4918025	0.4920237	0.4922397	0.4924506	0.4926564
2.5	0.4937903	0.4939634	0.4941323	0.4942969	0.4944574
2.6	0.4953388	0.4954729	0.4956035	0.4957308	0.4958547
2.7	0.4965330	0.4966358	0.4967359	0.4968333	0.4969280
2.8	0.4974449	0.4975229	0.4975988	0.4976726	0.4977443
2.9	0.4981342	0.4981929	0.4982498	0.4983052	0.4983589
3.0	0.4986501	0.4986938	0.4987361	0.4987772	0.4988171
3.1	0.4990324	0.4990646	0.4990957	0.4991260	0.4991553
3.2	0.4993129	0.4993363	0.4993590	0.4993810	0.4994024
3.3	0.4995166	0.4995335	0.4995499	0.4995658	0.4995811
3.4	0.4996631	0.4996752	0.4996869	0.4996982	0.4997091
3.5	0.4997674	0.4997759	0.4997842	0.4997922	0.4997999
3.6	0.4998409	0.4998469	0.4998527	0.4998583	0.4998637
3.7	0.4998922	0.4998964	0.4999004	0.4999043	0.4999080
3.8	0.4999277	0.4999305	0.4999333	0.4999359	0.4999385
3.9	0.4999519	0.4999539	0.4999557	0.4999575	0.4999593
4.0	0.4999683	0.4999696	0.4999709	0.4999721	0.4999733
4.1	0.4999793	0.4999802	0.4999811	0.4999819	0.4999826
4.2	0.4999867	0.4999872	0.4999878	0.4999883	0.4999888
4.3	0.4999915	0.4999918	0.4999922	0.4999925	0.4999929
4.4	0.4999946	0.4999948	0.4999951	0.4999953	0.4999955
4.5	0.4999966	0.4999968	0.4999969	0.4999971	0.4999972
4.6	0.4999979	0.4999980	0.4999981	0.4999982	0.4999983
4.7	0.4999987	0.4999988	0.4999988	0.4999989	0.4999989
4.8	0.4999992	0.4999992	0.4999993	0.4999993	0.4999994
4.9	0.4999995	0.4999995	0.4999996	0.4999996	0.4999996
5.0	0.4999997	0.4999997	0.4999997	0.4999998	0.4999998
5.1	0.4999998	0.4999998	0.4999998	0.4999999	0.4999999

0.05	0.06	0.07	0.08	0.09
0.4928572	0.4930531	0.4932443	0.4934309	0.4936128
0.4946139	0.4947664	0.4949151	0.4950600	0.4952012
0.4959754	0.4960930	0.4962074	0.4963189	0.4964274
0.4970202	0.4971099	0.4971972	0.4972821	0.4973646
0.4978140	0.4978818	0.4979476	0.4980116	0.4980738
0.4984111	0.4984618	0.4985110	0.4985588	0.4986051
0.4988558	0.4988933	0.4989297	0.4989650	0.4989992
0.4991836	0.4992112	0.4992378	0.4992636	0.4992886
0.4994230	0.4994429	0.4994623	0.4994810	0.4994991
0.4995959	0.4996103	0.4996242	0.4996376	0.4996505
0.4997197	0.4997299	0.4997398	0.4997493	0.4997585
0.4998074	0.4998146	0.4998215	0.4998282	0.4998347
0.4998689	0.4998739	0.4998787	0.4998834	0.4998879
0.4999116	0.4999150	0.4999184	0.4999216	0.4999247
0.4999409	0.4999433	0.4999456	0.4999478	0.4999499
0.4999609	0.4999625	0.4999641	0.4999655	0.4999670
0.4999744	0.4999755	0.4999765	0.4999775	0.4999784
0.4999834	0.4999841	0.4999848	0.4999854	0.4999861
0.4999893	0.4999898	0.4999902	0.4999907	0.4999911
0.4999932	0.4999935	0.4999938	0.4999941	0.4999943
0.4999957	0.4999959	0.4999961	0.4999963	0.4999964
0.4999973	0.4999974	0.4999976	0.4999977	0.4999978
0.4999983	0.4999984	0.4999985	0.4999986	0.4999986
0.4999990	0.4999990	0.4999991	0.4999991	0.4999992
0.4999994	0.4999994	0.4999994	0.4999995	0.4999995
0.4999996	0.4999996	0.4999997	0.4999997	0.4999997
0.4999998	0.4999998	0.4999998	0.4999998	0.4999998
0.4999999	0.4999999	0.4999999	0.4999999	0.4999999

APPENDIX B

OCCUPATION LISTING

Major Classifications and Occupational Titles

Management Occupations
Advertising and Promotions Managers
Marketing Managers
Sales Managers
Public Relations and Fundraising Managers
Administrative Services Managers
Computer and Information Systems Managers
Financial Managers
Industrial Production Managers
Purchasing Managers
Purchasing Managers
Transportation, Storage, and Distribution Managers
Compensation and Benefits Managers
Human Resources Managers
Training and Development Managers
Farmers, Ranchers, and Other Agricultural Managers
Construction Managers
Education Administrators, Preschool and Childcare Center/Program
Education Administrators, Elementary and Secondary School
Remaining Education Administrators
Architectural and Engineering Managers
Food Service Managers
Lodging Managers
Medical and Health Services Managers

Natural Sciences Managers
Social and Community Service Managers
Emergency Management Directors
Remaining Managers
Chief Executives
General and Operations Managers

Business and Financial Operations Occupations
Buyers and Purchasing Agents, Farm Products
Wholesale and Retail Buyers, Except Farm Products
Purchasing Agents, Except Wholesale, Retail, and Farm Products
Claims Adjusters, Examiners, and Investigators
Insurance Appraisers, Auto Damage
Compliance Officers
Cost Estimators
Farm Labor Contractors
Remaining Human Resources, Training, and Labor Relations
Specialists
Logisticians
Management Analysts
Meeting, Convention, and Event Planners
Compensation, Benefits, and Job Analysis Specialists
Training and Development Specialists
Market Research Analysts and Marketing Specialists
Remaining Business Operations Specialists
Accountants and Auditors
Appraisers and Assessors of Real Estate
Budget Analysts
Credit Analysts
Financial Analysts
Personal Financial Advisors
Insurance Underwriters
Financial Examiners
Credit Counselors
Loan Officers
Remaining Financial Specialists

Computer and Mathematical Occupations
Computer and Information Research Scientists
Computer Systems Analysts

Computer Programmers
Software Developers, Applications
Software Developers, Systems Software
Database Administrators
Network and Computer Systems Administrators*
Computer Support Specialists
Information Security Analysts, Web Developers, and Computer
Network Architects
Remaining Computer Occupations
Operations Research Analysts
Statisticians

Architecture and Engineering Occupations
Architects, Except Landscape and Naval
Landscape Architects
Cartographers and Photogrammetrists
Surveyors
Aerospace Engineers
Agricultural Engineers
Biomedical Engineers
Chemical Engineers
Civil Engineers
Computer Hardware Engineers
Electrical Engineers
Electronics Engineers, Except Computer
Environmental Engineers
Health and Safety Engineers, Except Mining Safety Engineers and
Inspectors
Industrial Engineers
Marine Engineers and Naval Architects
Materials Engineers
Mechanical Engineers
Mining and Geological Engineers, Including Mining Safety
Engineers
Nuclear Engineers
Petroleum Engineers
Remaining Engineers
Architectural and Civil Drafters
Electrical and Electronics Drafters
Mechanical Drafters

Remaining Drafters
Aerospace Engineering and Operations Technicians
Civil Engineering Technicians
Electrical and Electronics Engineering Technicians
Electro-Mechanical Technicians
Environmental Engineering Technicians
Industrial Engineering Technicians
Mechanical Engineering Technicians
Remaining Engineering Technicians, Except Drafters
Surveying and Mapping Technicians

Life, Physical, and Social Science Occupations
Animal Scientists
Food Scientists and Technologists
Soil and Plant Scientists
Biochemists and Biophysicists
Microbiologists
Remaining Biological Scientists
Foresters
Epidemiologists
Medical Scientists, Except Epidemiologists
Remaining Life Scientists
Physicists
Atmospheric and Space Scientists
Chemists
Materials Scientists
Environmental Scientists and Specialists, Including Health
Geoscientists, Except Hydrologists and Geographers
Remaining Physical Scientists
Economists
Clinical, Counseling, and School Psychologists
Remaining Psychologists
Agricultural and Food Science Technicians
Biological Technicians
Chemical Technicians
Geological and Petroleum Technicians
Environmental Science and Protection Technicians, Including Health
Forest and Conservation Technicians
Remaining Life, Physical, and Social Science Technicians

Community and Social Service Occupations
Substance Abuse and Behavioral Disorder Counselors
Educational, Guidance, School, and Vocational Counselors
Marriage and Family Therapists
Mental Health Counselors
Rehabilitation Counselors
Remaining Counselors
Child, Family, and School Social Workers
Healthcare Social Workers
Mental Health and Substance Abuse Social Workers
Remaining Social Workers
Health Educators
Probation Officers and Correctional Treatment Specialists
Social and Human Service Assistants
Remaining Community and Social Service Specialists
Clergy
Directors, Religious Activities and Education
Remaining Religious Workers

Legal Occupations
Lawyers
Paralegals and Legal Assistants
Title Examiners, Abstractors, and Searchers
Remaining Legal Support Workers
Education, Training, and Library Occupations
Vocational Education Teachers, Postsecondary
Preschool Teachers, Except Special Education
Elementary School Teachers, Except Special Education
Middle School Teachers, Except Special and Career/Technical Education
Secondary School Teachers, Except Special and Career/Technical Education
Career/Technical Education Teachers, Secondary School
Special Education Teachers, Preschool, Kindergarten, and Elementary School
Special Education Teachers, Middle School
Special Education Teachers, Secondary School
Adult Basic and Secondary Education and Literacy Teachers and Instructors
Self-Enrichment Education Teachers

Remaining Teachers and Instructors
Archivists
Librarians
Library Technicians
Farm and Home Management Advisors
Instructional Coordinators
Teacher Assistants
Remaining Education, Training, and Library Workers

Arts, Design, Entertainment, Sports, and Media Occupations
Art Directors
Craft Artists
Fine Artists, Including Painters, Sculptors, and Illustrators
Multimedia Artists and Animators
Commercial and Industrial Designers
Fashion Designers
Floral Designers
Graphic Designers
Interior Designers
Merchandise Displayers and Window Trimmers
Set and Exhibit Designers
Remaining Designers
Producers and Directors
Coaches and Scouts
Dancers
Musicians and Singers
Remaining Entertainers and Performers, Sports and Related Workers
Radio and Television Announcers
Public Address System and Other Announcers
Broadcast News Analysts
Reporters and Correspondents
Public Relations Specialists
Editors
Technical Writers
Writers and Authors
Interpreters and Translators
Interpreters and Translators
Audio and Video Equipment Technicians
Remaining Media and Communication Workers
Broadcast Technicians

Sound Engineering Technicians
Photographers
Camera Operators, Television, Video, and Motion Picture
Film and Video Editors
Remaining Media and Communication Equipment Workers

Healthcare Practitioners and Technical Occupations
Dentists, General
Dietitians and Nutritionists
Optometrists
Pharmacists
Family and General Practitioners
Pediatricians, General
Psychiatrists
Remaining Physicians and Surgeons
Physician Assistants
Registered Nurses
Occupational Therapists
Physical Therapists
Recreational Therapists
Respiratory Therapists
Speech-Language Pathologists
Remaining Therapists
Veterinarians
Audiologists
Remaining Health Diagnosing and Treating Practitioners
Medical and Clinical Laboratory Technologists
Medical and Clinical Laboratory Technicians
Dental Hygienists
Cardiovascular Technologists and Technicians
Nuclear Medicine Technologists
Radiologic Technologists and Technicians
Emergency Medical Technicians and Paramedics
Dietetic Technicians
Pharmacy Technicians
Psychiatric Technicians
Respiratory Therapy Technicians
Veterinary Technologists and Technicians
Licensed Practical and Licensed Vocational Nurses
Medical Records and Health Information Technicians

Opticians, Dispensing
Orthotists and Prosthetists
Remaining Health Technologists and Technicians
Occupational Health and Safety Specialists
Occupational Health and Safety Technicians
Remaining Healthcare Practitioners and Technical Workers

Healthcare Support Occupations
Home Health Aides
Nursing Aides, Orderlies, and Attendants
Psychiatric Aides
Occupational Therapy Assistants
Occupational Therapy Aides
Physical Therapist Assistants
Physical Therapist Aides
Massage Therapists
Dental Assistants
Medical Assistants
Medical Equipment Preparers
Medical Transcriptionists
Pharmacy Aides
Veterinary Assistants and Laboratory Animal Caretakers
Remaining Healthcare Support Workers

Protective Service Occupations
First-Line Supervisors of Fire Fighting and Prevention Workers
Remaining First-Line Supervisors of Protective Service Workers
Firefighters
Fire Inspectors and Investigators
Correctional Officers and Jailers
Private Detectives and Investigators
Security Guards
Crossing Guards
Lifeguards, Ski Patrol, and Other Recreational Protective Service
Workers
Remaining Protective Service Workers

Food Preparation and Serving Related Occupations
Chefs and Head Cooks
First-Line Supervisors of Food Preparation and Serving Workers

Cooks, Fast Food
Cooks, Institution and Cafeteria
Cooks, Restaurant
Cooks, Short Order
Remaining Cooks
Food Preparation Workers
Bartenders
Combined Food Preparation and Serving Workers, Including Fast Food
Counter Attendants, Cafeteria, Food Concession, and Coffee Shop
Waiters and Waitresses
Food Servers, Non-restaurant
Dining Room and Cafeteria Attendants and Bartender Helpers
Dishwashers
Hosts and Hostesses, Restaurant, Lounge, and Coffee Shop
Remaining Food Preparation and Serving Related Workers

Building and Grounds Cleaning and Maintenance Occupations
First-Line Supervisors of Housekeeping and Janitorial Workers
First-Line Supervisors of Landscaping, Lawn Service, and Grounds keeping Workers
Janitors and Cleaners, Except Maids and Housekeeping Cleaners
Maids and Housekeeping Cleaners
Remaining Building Cleaning Workers
Pest Control Workers
Landscaping and Grounds keeping Workers
Pesticide Handlers, Sprayers, and Applicators, Vegetation
Tree Trimmers and Pruners
Remaining Grounds Maintenance Workers

Personal Care and Service Occupations
First-Line Supervisors of Personal Service Workers
Gaming and Sports Book Writers and Runners
Motion Picture Projectionists
Ushers, Lobby Attendants, and Ticket Takers
Locker Room, Coatroom, and Dressing Room Attendants
Remaining Entertainment Attendants and Related Workers
Barbers
Hairdressers, Hairstylists, and Cosmetologists
Manicurists and Pedicurists

Skincare Specialists
Baggage Porters and Bellhops
Concierges
Tour Guides and Escorts
Childcare Workers
Personal Care Aides
Fitness Trainers and Aerobics Instructors
Recreation Workers
Residential Advisors
Remaining Personal Care and Service Workers

Sales and Related Occupations
First-Line Supervisors of Retail Sales Workers
First-Line Supervisors of Non-Retail Sales Workers
Cashiers
Counter and Rental Clerks
Parts Salespersons
Retail Salespersons
Advertising Sales Agents
Insurance Sales Agents
Securities, Commodities, and Financial Services Sales Agents
Travel Agents
Remaining Sales Representatives, Services
Sales Representatives, Wholesale and Manufacturing, Technical and Scientific Products
Sales Representatives, Wholesale and Manufacturing, Except Technical and Scientific Products
Demonstrators and Product Promoters
Real Estate Brokers
Real Estate Sales Agents
Sales Engineers
Telemarketers
Door-to-Door Sales Workers, News and Street Vendors, and Related Workers
Remaining Sales and Related Workers

Office and Administrative Support Occupations
First-Line Supervisors of Office and Administrative Support Workers
Switchboard Operators, Including Answering Service

Telephone Operators
Remaining Communications Equipment Operators
Bill and Account Collectors
Billing and Posting Clerks
Bookkeeping, Accounting, and Auditing Clerks
Payroll and Timekeeping Clerks
Procurement Clerks
Tellers
Brokerage Clerks
Correspondence Clerks
Credit Authorizers, Checkers, and Clerks
Customer Service Representatives
Eligibility Interviewers, Government Programs
File Clerks
Hotel, Motel, and Resort Desk Clerks
Interviewers, Except Eligibility and Loan
Library Assistants, Clerical
Loan Interviewers and Clerks
New Accounts Clerks
Order Clerks
Human Resources Assistants, Except Payroll and Timekeeping
Receptionists and Information Clerks
Reservation and Transportation Ticket Agents and Travel Clerks
Remaining Information and Record Clerks
Cargo and Freight Agents
Couriers and Messengers
Police, Fire, and Ambulance Dispatchers
Dispatchers, Except Police, Fire, and Ambulance
Meter Readers, Utilities
Production, Planning, and Expediting Clerks
Shipping, Receiving, and Traffic Clerks
Stock Clerks and Order Fillers
Weighers, Measurers, Checkers, and Samplers, Recordkeeping
Executive Secretaries and Executive Administrative Assistants
Legal Secretaries
Medical Secretaries
Secretaries and Administrative Assistants, Except Legal, Medical, and Executive
Computer Operators
Data Entry Keyers

Word Processors and Typists
Desktop Publishers
Insurance Claims and Policy Processing Clerks
Mail Clerks and Mail Machine Operators, Except Postal Service
Office Clerks, General
Office Machine Operators, Except Computer
Proofreaders and Copy Markers
Proofreaders and Copy Markers
Statistical Assistants
Remaining Office and Administrative Support Workers

Farming, Fishing, and Forestry Occupations
First-Line Supervisors of Farming, Fishing, and Forestry Workers
Agricultural Inspectors
Animal Breeders
Graders and Sorters, Agricultural Products
Agricultural Equipment Operators
Farm workers and Laborers, Crop, Nursery, and Greenhouse
Farm workers, Farm, Ranch, and Aquacultural Animals
Remaining Agricultural Workers
Fishers and Related Fishing Workers
Fallers
Logging Equipment Operators
Log Graders and Scalers
Remaining Logging Workers

Construction and Extraction Occupations
First-Line Supervisors of Construction Trades and Extraction
Workers
Boilermakers
Brick masons and Block masons
Stonemasons
Carpenters
Carpet Installers
Floor Layers, Except Carpet, Wood, and Hard Tiles
Floor Sanders and Finishers
Tile and Marble Setters
Cement Masons and Concrete Finishers
Terrazzo Workers and Finishers
Construction Laborers

Paving, Surfacing, and Tamping Equipment Operators
Pile-Driver Operators
Operating Engineers and Other Construction Equipment Operators
Drywall and Ceiling Tile Installers
Tapers
Electricians
Glaziers
Insulation Workers, Floor, Ceiling, and Wall
Insulation Workers, Mechanical
Painters, Construction and Maintenance
Paperhangers
Pipe layers
Plumbers, Pipe fitters, and Steamfitters
Plasterers and Stucco Masons
Reinforcing Iron and Rebar Workers
Roofers
Sheet Metal Workers
Structural Iron and Steel Workers
Helpers—Brick masons, Block masons, Stonemasons, and Tile and Marble Setters
Helpers--Carpenters
Helpers--Electricians
Helpers--Painters, Paperhangers, Plasterers, and Stucco Masons
Helpers—Pipe layers, Plumbers, Pipe fitters, and Steamfitters
Helpers--Roofers
Remaining Helpers, Construction Trades
Construction and Building Inspectors
Elevator Installers and Repairers
Fence Erectors
Hazardous Materials Removal Workers
Rail-Track Laying and Maintenance Equipment Operators
Septic Tank Servicers and Sewer Pipe Cleaners
Segmental Pavers
Remaining Construction and Related Workers
Derrick Operators, Oil and Gas
Rotary Drill Operators, Oil and Gas
Service Unit Operators, Oil, Gas, and Mining
Earth Drillers, Except Oil and Gas
Explosives Workers, Ordnance Handling Experts, and Blasters
Remaining Mining Machine Operators

Rock Splitters, Quarry
Roustabouts, Oil and Gas
Helpers--Extraction Workers
Remaining Extraction Workers

Installation, Maintenance, and Repair Occupations

First-Line Supervisors of Mechanics, Installers, and Repairers
Computer, Automated Teller, and Office Machine Repairers
Radio, Cellular, and Tower Equipment Installers and Repairs
Telecommunications Equipment Installers and Repairers, Except
Line Installers
Avionics Technicians
Electric Motor, Power Tool, and Related Repairers
Electrical and Electronics Installers and Repairers, Transportation
Equipment
Electrical and Electronics Repairers, Commercial and Industrial
Equipment
Electrical and Electronics Repairers, Powerhouse, Substation, and
Relay
Electronic Equipment Installers and Repairers, Motor Vehicles
Electronic Home Entertainment Equipment Installers and Repairers
Security and Fire Alarm Systems Installers
Aircraft Mechanics and Service Technicians
Automotive Body and Related Repairers
Automotive Glass Installers and Repairers
Automotive Service Technicians and Mechanics
Bus and Truck Mechanics and Diesel Engine Specialists
Farm Equipment Mechanics and Service Technicians
Mobile Heavy Equipment Mechanics, Except Engines
Rail Car Repairers
Motorboat Mechanics and Service Technicians
Motorcycle Mechanics
Outdoor Power Equipment and Other Small Engine Mechanics
Bicycle Repairers
Recreational Vehicle Service Technicians
Tire Repairers and Changers
Mechanical Door Repairers
Control and Valve Installers and Repairers, Except Mechanical Door
Heating, Air Conditioning, and Refrigeration Mechanics and
Installers

Home Appliance Repairers
Industrial Machinery Mechanics
Maintenance Workers, Machinery
Millwrights
Refractory Materials Repairers, Except Brick Masons
Electrical Power-Line Installers and Repairers
Telecommunications Line Installers and Repairers
Camera and Photographic Equipment Repairers
Medical Equipment Repairers
Musical Instrument Repairers and Tuners
Watch Repairers
Remaining Precision Instrument and Equipment Repairers
Maintenance and Repair Workers, General
Coin, Vending, and Amusement Machine Servicers and Repairers
Commercial Divers
Fabric Menders, Except Garment
Locksmiths and Safe Repairers
Manufactured Building and Mobile Home Installers
Riggers
Signal and Track Switch Repairers
Helpers--Installation, Maintenance, and Repair Workers
Remaining Installation, Maintenance, and Repair Workers

Production Occupations
First-Line Supervisors of Production and Operating Workers
Aircraft Structure, Surfaces, Rigging, and Systems Assemblers
Electrical and Electronic Equipment Assemblers
Electromechanical Equipment Assemblers
Engine and Other Machine Assemblers
Structural Metal Fabricators and Fitters
Fiberglass Laminators and Fabricators
Team Assemblers
Timing Device Assemblers and Adjusters
Remaining Assemblers and Fabricators
Bakers
Butchers and Meat Cutters
Meat, Poultry, and Fish Cutters and Trimmers
Slaughterers and Meat Packers
Food and Tobacco Roasting, Baking, and Drying Machine Operators
and Tenders

Food Batch Makers
Food Cooking Machine Operators and Tenders
Computer-Controlled Machine Tool Operators, Metal and Plastic
Computer Numerically Controlled Machine Tool Programmers,
Metal and Plastic
Extruding and Drawing Machine Setters, Operators, and Tenders,
Metal and Plastic
Forging Machine Setters, Operators, and Tenders, Metal and Plastic
Rolling Machine Setters, Operators, and Tenders, Metal and Plastic
Cutting, Punching, and Press Machine Setters, Operators, and
Tenders, Metal and Plastic
Drilling and Boring Machine Tool Setters, Operators, and Tenders,
Metal and Plastic
Grinding, Lapping, Polishing, and Buffing Machine Tool Setters,
Operators, and Tenders, Metal and Plastic
Lathe and Turning Machine Tool Setters, Operators, and Tenders,
Metal and Plastic
Milling and Planing Machine Setters, Operators, and Tenders, Metal
and Plastic
Machinists
Metal-Refining Furnace Operators and Tenders
Pourers and Casters, Metal
Model Makers, Metal and Plastic
Patternmakers, Metal and Plastic
Foundry Mold and Core Makers
Molding, Core making, and Casting Machine Setters, Operators, and
Tenders, Metal and Plastic
Multiple Machine Tool Setters, Operators, and Tenders, Metal and
Plastic
Tool and Die Makers
Welders, Cutters, Solderers, and Brazers
Welding, Soldering, and Brazing Machine Setters, Operators, and
Tenders
Heat Treating Equipment Setters, Operators, and Tenders, Metal and
Plastic
Layout Workers, Metal and Plastic
Plating and Coating Machine Setters, Operators, and Tenders, Metal
and Plastic
Tool Grinders, Filers, and Sharpeners
Remaining Metal Workers and Plastic Workers

Prepress Technicians and Workers
Printing Press Operators
Print Binding and Finishing Workers
Laundry and Dry-Cleaning Workers
Pressers, Textile, Garment, and Related Materials
Sewing Machine Operators
Shoe and Leather Workers and Repairers
Sewers, Hand
Tailors, Dressmakers, and Custom Sewers
Textile Bleaching and Dyeing Machine Operators and Tenders
Textile Cutting Machine Setters, Operators, and Tenders
Textile Knitting and Weaving Machine Setters, Operators, and Tenders
Textile Winding, Twisting, and Drawing Out Machine Setters, Operators, and Tenders
Extruding and Forming Machine Setters, Operators, and Tenders, Synthetic and Glass Fibers
Fabric and Apparel Patternmakers
Upholsterers
Remaining Textile, Apparel, and Furnishings Workers
Cabinetmakers and Bench Carpenters
Furniture Finishers
Model Makers, Wood
Patternmakers, Wood
Sawing Machine Setters, Operators, and Tenders, Wood
Woodworking Machine Setters, Operators, and Tenders, Except Sawing
Remaining Woodworkers
Power Plant Operators
Stationary Engineers and Boiler Operators
Water and Wastewater Treatment Plant and System Operators
Chemical Plant and System Operators
Gas Plant Operators
Petroleum Pump System Operators, Refinery Operators, and Gaugers
Remaining Plant and System Operators
Chemical Equipment Operators and Tenders
Separating, Filtering, Clarifying, Precipitating, and Still Machine Setters, Operators, and Tenders
Crushing, Grinding, and Polishing Machine Setters, Operators, and Tenders

Grinding and Polishing Workers, Hand
Mixing and Blending Machine Setters, Operators, and Tenders
Cutters and Trimmers, Hand
Cutting and Slicing Machine Setters, Operators, and Tenders
Extruding, Forming, Pressing, and Compacting Machine Setters, Operators, and Tenders
Furnace, Kiln, Oven, Drier, and Kettle Operators and Tenders
Inspectors, Testers, Sorters, Samplers, and Weighers
Jewelers, Precious Stone, and Metal Workers
Dental Laboratory Technicians
Medical Appliance Technicians
Ophthalmic Laboratory Technicians
Packaging and Filling Machine Operators and Tenders
Coating, Painting, and Spraying Machine Setters, Operators, and Tenders
Painters, Transportation Equipment
Painting, Coating, and Decorating Workers
Semiconductor Processors
Photographic Process Workers and Processing Machine Operators
Adhesive Bonding Machine Operators and Tenders
Cleaning, Washing, and Metal Pickling Equipment Operators and Tenders
Cooling and Freezing Equipment Operators and Tenders
Etchers and Engravers
Molders, Shapers, and Casters, Except Metal and Plastic
Paper Goods Machine Setters, Operators, and Tenders
Tire Builders
Helpers--Production Workers
Remaining Production Workers

Transportation and Material Moving Occupations
Aircraft Cargo Handling Supervisors
First-Line Supervisors of Helpers, Laborers, and Material Movers, Hand
First-Line Supervisors of Transportation and Material-Moving Machine and Vehicle Operators
Airline Pilots, Copilots, and Flight Engineers
Commercial Pilots
Air Traffic Controllers
Airfield Operations Specialists

Flight Attendants
Bus Drivers, Transit and Intercity
Bus Drivers, School or Special Client
Driver/Sales Workers
Heavy and Tractor-Trailer Truck Drivers
Light Truck or Delivery Services Drivers
Taxi Drivers and Chauffeurs
Remaining Motor Vehicle Operators
Rail Yard Engineers, Dinkey Operators, and Hostlers
Sailors and Marine Oilers
Captains, Mates, and Pilots of Water Vessels
Motorboat Operators
Ship Engineers
Parking Lot Attendants
Automotive and Watercraft Service Attendants
Transportation Inspectors
Transportation Attendants, Except Flight Attendants
Remaining Transportation Workers
Conveyor Operators and Tenders
Crane and Tower Operators
Dredge Operators
Excavating and Loading Machine and Dragline Operators
Hoist and Winch Operators
Industrial Truck and Tractor Operators
Cleaners of Vehicles and Equipment
Laborers and Freight, Stock, and Material Movers, Hand
Machine Feeders and Off Bearers
Packers and Packagers, Hand
Gas Compressor and Gas Pumping Station Operators
Pump Operators, Except Wellhead Pumpers
Wellhead Pumpers
Refuse and Recyclable Material Collectors
Refuse and Recyclable Material Collectors
Tank Car, Truck, and Ship Loaders
Remaining Material Moving Workers

ABOUT THE AUTHOR

Dr. Joseph Bounds earned his B. S. at Northern Michigan University, M. S. at California State, and DBA with Argosy University with a management concentration. He is a senior member of the American Society for Quality and holds three certifications, among them a Six Sigma Black Belt. Over his career, Dr. Bounds has worked in several industries and held various positions from equipment operator to department manager and also teaches at local community colleges on an as needed basis. Since the economic downturn in 2008, he has worked primarily as a private contractor in the quality field with industry. During his doctoral studies he became interested in developing a metric for defining "excessive" executive compensation, basing his dissertation on this ground breaking research.